ICELAND YESTERDAY AND TODAY

by Horace Leaf

UNDER THE SOUTHERN CROSS

ICELAND YESTERDAY AND TODAY

by

HORACE LEAF
F.R.G.S

LONDON

GEORGE ALLEN & UNWIN LTD

Ruskin House Museum Street

FIRST PUBLISHED IN 1949

PRINTED IN GREAT BRITAIN
in 13 point Walbaum type
BY CAINES OF PLAISTOW
LONDON

DEDICATION

To my Icelandic friends

FOREWORD

In presenting this book to the public I should be failing in my duty if I did not pay tribute to those Icelanders whose unremitting kindness made the work possible.

First among them must be mentioned Mr. Snaebjorn Jónsson who read the MS and made suggestions and corrections without which the book would have been much less valuable.

It would be difficult to mention all who rendered assistance, but special regard must be paid Mrs. Halldora Sigurjonson, without whose advocacy my visit to Iceland might never have been made, and who, with Mrs. Ólof Pjetursson drew my attention to many interesting features of their country.

The invaluable services of Mr. Sigbjorn Armann and Mr. Niculas Fridricksson have been duly acknowledged in the book. My thanks are also due to Mrs. Sigrid Holbeck for her correspondence after my return to Scotland, to Professor Matthias Thórdarson for his services to me at the National Museum, Reykjavík, and to Mr. Gudmundur S. Hofdal for useful information.

My thanks are also owing Mrs. M. Bogason in whose home much of this book was written. It is lamentable that I am unable again to thank the late Mr. Pall S. Thormar and the late Mr. Gudjon Jónsson for their encouragement and assistance.

CONTENTS

ILLUSTRATIONS

Chapter 1

TO ICELAND

MY first acquaintance with Icelanders was at Wynyard, Saskatchewan, Canada, in the summer of 1929. They were a farming community, wringing a precarious living from the soil, in a climate sometimes warmer and sometimes colder than that of their native land. All of them bore the impress of their arduous tasks; but they were an intelligent people, deeply interested in psychological, philosophical and religious problems. It was this that marked them off from the great majority of farmers in the land of their adoption. Canadians are, as a whole, a materialistically-minded people, filled with a belief in the physical greatness of their country and enamoured of its business and industrial prospects.

In the Icelandic settlement at Wynyard nearly everybody seemed keenly interested in intellectual pursuits, and through this found no small relief from the onerous demands of their daily life. It was obvious that they had a better mental background than most Canadian immigrants.

I had ample opportunity, alas, of seeing how these simple, honest, industrious people reacted to misfortune, thus testing the value of their philosophy. The summer was well advanced when I arrived at Wynyard, and there were excellent prospects of a first-class harvest. The weather had been so good that if it had continued all corn crops would have been rated as first-class. Unfortunately, in the middle of July a severe frost lasting several days set in, and everything was ruined. These good people had to watch the results of their labour disappear, and in the end they cleared their fields by burning their crops.

A severer test of morale would be difficult to find; but they yielded to the inevitable with philosophic calm, hardly a grumble coming from them. Eventually many of them packed up and went farther west, where the chances of a repetition of their misfortune were considerably reduced. This stoicism was amazing and could not fail to win admiration.

Practically all these people had been born in Iceland, and they bore the impress of their native environment. Not that they were a rugged-looking people; on the contrary many of them were blond, tall and cheerful-looking, although they were, I thought, neither bouyant nor vivacious. They were natural optimists, a characteristic which showed through a certain quietness which might have been mistaken for depression. It is obvious, from such contradictory terms, that to describe the Icelandic national disposition is not easy, and one must visit Iceland to realise the reason why.

I eventually sailed for Iceland itself on the S.S. *Horsa*, 29th May, 1946. The trip was scheduled to take about three and a half days, but we struck one of the worst storms for several years and reached Reykjavík about twenty-four hours late. There were three Icelanders among the eight passengers, and they confirmed my previous opinion of them. Two were quiet, gentle and unassuming; the third a talkative young woman who had married an Englishman of whom she was exceedingly proud. In appearance and manners they were indistinguishable from the British passengers, with whom they mixed on friendly terms. There was evidently no feeling of that inferiority that one might expect from a race numbering only 130,000, and situated on an island so far north as to be almost on the edge of the world.

Whoever has read the earlier sagas will readily understand the natural confidence of Icelanders. They are the direct descendants for the main part of the old Vikings. We know what these adventurers looked like, dressed picturesquely while driving their artistic galleys through unknown seas, bent on piracy. They were notably fierce and brave, dealing out death as readily as they received it. Time and circumstance have, of course, brought about changes. For hundreds of years the descendants of these intrepid warriors have devoted themselves to farming and fishing, maintaining in the meantime, no militant forces.

The result is that they have turned their energies to peaceful pursuits, increased their social amenities, and developed a love of literature, for which they are justly famous.

I had already had the good fortune to make the acquaintance of two highly educated Icelanders in London. One was the well-known Rev. Haraldur Nielsson, Professor of Theology at Reykjavík University; the other Mr. Snaebjörn Jónsson, a noted author and translator. But one way and another I was still uncertain what I might find in Iceland, although I had every reason to expect the best.

I knew that it possessed the heaviest reading public in the world; that the publication of books there in proportion to population, greatly exceeds that of any other country. For instance, in Iceland there is one publication to every 466 inhabitants, compared with Britain's one to 3,205 and the United States' one to every 12,497. Their high standard of general education doubtless increases their sense of personal worth, and this so jarred on one American engineer that I met in Reykjavík, that he irritably assured me that "one would think by their behaviour that Iceland has a population as large as the United States or Russia."

The first view of the coast of Iceland is attractive because of its grim, rugged appearance. The irregular shores, almost mountain-lined, seem to cast a spiritual gloom on minds used to softer and more congenial scenery. Its uneven coastline is dual in character, being honeycombed with bays and inlets, while numerous mountains rise in varied splendour sharply from the very border inland. Mount Hekla, one of the most active volcanoes in the world, stands like a mighty sentinel, whose helmet of snow can be seen for hours towering above the horizon. Nearby what at first seems to be a peculiar layer of snow casts a white cloud over the scene, but after a while it is seen to alter its shape and height, and is found to be a cloud of steam rising from one of the numerous fumaroles so liberally scattered about the island.

It is the Westmen Islands which first capture the visitor's gaze, and they remain in view almost indefinitely as the ship steams westward. For my part, land was welcome enough, as to come under its shelter was to abate the stormy seas which had for four days battered our labouring ship, and gave her a peaceful ending to a savage voyage. But all discomfort was soon forgotten as we watched the ever-changing shore, revealing here and there a solitary farm, or a small cluster of houses, hardly deserving the name of hamlet, but in Iceland called a town. I soon concluded that among the many countries that I had seen none resembled Iceland, a conclusion fully justified after I had travelled through almost every part of it except the interior.

From the moment one passes Eldey, a large solitary rock, well-known to bird-lovers and egg-collectors, and rounds the sharp headland, Skagaflös, and enters Faxaflói or Faxa Bay, on the west shore of which stands Snaefelljökull, the scenery becomes more intimate and charming. It was a peculiar charm, overshadowed at the moment by the ominous snowcapped mountains, some of which, like Esja, lay sprawling giantlike on the shore.

The sun was shining with fitful gleams as we approached Reykjavík, and the sombreness of the scene could not be disregarded. Over everything seemed to hover an aura which on closer inspection was caused by vague clouds of colour of darker hues. In common with most mountain ranges, those of Iceland are often suffused by blue mists which every now and then are pierced by the rays of the sun. It was early June and Iceland's summer had begun, yet everywhere one looked mantles of snow covered the mountain tops and sides.

It was intriguing to think that on this same superb scene, in the year 874, gazed Ingólfur Arnarson, the true founder of the country. The passengers lining the sides of the ship and watching the distant shore must have beheld the very spot on which the slaves of this notable man found the main pillars of his house and established Reykjavík. The exact spot is not known. Ingólfur, deeply attached to his pagan faith, had thrown these posts overboard as he approached Iceland, in the full belief that his gods would direct them to the spot where they desired him to reside; and from that simple homestead has grown the capital city, Reykjavík, named after Ingólfur's own house, which means "steam," because of the hot springs in the vicinity.

Ingólfur was so satisfied with the choice of the gods that he proceeded to encourage others to follow him, and from Norway, the land of his birth, from England, Ireland and Scotland flowed a steady stream of immigrants. Within sixty years the land was pretty well occupied. Previous to moving to Rekjavík, Ingólfur Arnarson resided at Arnarhóll, a charming plain about thirty miles east of Reykjavík, extending from the foot of a range of mountains southward to the sea. I visited this part of the country frequently, and stayed for some time at the foot of the mountain close to which Ingólfur resided for three years, and named after him. I wondered why he left such a charming spot, with its rich arable lands, for the broken lava fields round Reykjavík. The reason became apparent, however, when it was pointed out that this part of the country had no harbour. Ingólfur and his gods made no mistake.

The honour of discovering Iceland fell to Naddodd, a famous pirate who, in 861, was driven there by a tempest while on his way to the Faroes. Naddodd gave a good account of the country, notwithstanding that he found it covered with so much snow that he called it Snaeland. His description induced Garder Svavarsson, a Swede, to visit it in 864, at a place called Skjalfjaudi, where the town of

Húsavik now stands. I stayed in Húsavik several days. Thirty years ago it consisted merely of a few scattered farms, but today it is a flourishing town with a population of more than 1,200. The slow growth of this town will give an idea of how Iceland has been tabooed by emigrants; who have preferred to go to colder and less propitious climes, largely because the name Iceland is unattractive.

The next adventurer was Flóki Vilgardarson, a Viking, after whom Iceland was named. Flóki sailed before the compass had been discovered, and found the island by releasing a raven when he thought he was in its vicinity, hoping that the bird would direct its course there. But it flew towards Norway, from whence Flóki had come. A second raven when released merely returned to the ship; but on releasing a third a few days later Flóki was gratified to observe it fly towards his destination. It is known, however, that before any of these explorers reached Iceland, it had been visited occasionally by sailors, probably from Ireland and Scotland, as they left evidence of their presence in the form of various religious objects belonging to the Roman Catholic faith.

It was obvious when the *Horsa* docked at Reykjavík that there was nothing primitive about the city. The docks were modern, the people well-dressed, many of the young people who stood watching our arrival showing a predilection for American styles of dress. The front was well stocked with American motor cars, many of them quite new and all rather imposing. There was plenty of colour too, which was very refreshing after more than four days of drab skies and leaden seas. I disembarked with no small pleasure, to be greeted by a company of Icelanders who had come to welcome me. All of them spoke English, some so well that it might have been their native tongue; and as there was nothing exotic about their appearance, I felt thoroughly at home.

It was evident that this isolated city was much nearer London and Paris than I had expected, and by the time I reached the hotel all illusions of igloos had been completely

1. REYKJAVIK 1946

This picture is taken from West to East and shows the Western and Middle part of the Town Left hand lower corner Ship Repair and Mechanical shops

2. REYKJAVIK

above : *Municipal Houses* ; below : *a Children's School*

dissipated. Any Briton or American could feel immediately at home in Reykjavík, although the people were somewhat retiring where strangers were concerned. This manifestation of good manners on the part of Icelanders is often mistaken for unfriendliness, especially by Americans who are notably free and easy with strangers; and I soon found that our own sailors, who often visited the harbour for a day or so, were unfavourably impressed by this reserve. The fact is Icelanders are shy, but when the barriers have broken down they prove to be an extremely friendly people.

There is, of course, nothing on a big scale in this city of 48,000 inhabitants; and there was a fair share of the old with the modern in the buildings. It is impossible to speak of the ancient in a land which possesses no prehistoric remains, and owing to the temporary nature of the materials used in the past in the erection of buildings, any edifice more than one hundred years old is rare.

Many of the shops and factories were of recent structure, and later on I was to see how well the city was being developed. For the moment one was struck with the layout of the streets, some of which were narrow, most of them unpaved, while many of the houses were painted red, green, cream, grey, blue and white. In the older part of the city, and that lies near the centre, many of the houses were of wood, with corrugated iron covering the walls and roofs. Originally Reykjavík could not have been laid out according to a plan, the houses springing up much as they did in English towns, although on the whole the streets of Reykjavík are less winding. An artist might well be pleased by the colourfulness of the place, but would find insufficient of the beautiful and quaint to wish to paint it. As a matter of fact, even Icelandic artists seldom devote their talent in this way.

Relative to the total population of the country Reykjavík may claim to be the largest city in the world, as probably more than one-third of the people live there, and it is growing rapidly. Another of its outstanding characteristics is that, in addition to being up-to-date in sanitation and hygiene, it is almost entirely supplied with central heating by the municipality, which has utilised hot springs for this purpose.

CHAPTER 2

REYKJAVÍK

REYKJAVÍK rapidly grows upon the visitor, and after a short time one feels not that Reykjavík is too small, but that other metropolises are too large. There is something decidedly friendly about the place and he soons feels at home in it.

It is, of course, the seat of Government and contains most of the principal buildings, including the Parliament house, the Cathedral and the University. Situated between and upon two hills, it is surrounded partly by a distant range of mountains and partly by the sea. To the north and north-east lie the much admired mountains Akrafjall and Esja, the latter said to derive its name from an Irishwoman who once farmed near it. The flat summit of this eminence, which lies recumbent between two small fjörds, is often obscured by low-lying clouds, and after a brief fall of snow looks lovely in its white cloak. Behind Akrafjall and Esja stands Skardsheidi, a mighty range of hills rearing their sharp peaks proudly towards the sky. This range is always partly covered with snow, a fact equally true of most of the mountain ranges in Iceland, unless the summer is unusually warm.

Whoever has lived in mountainous countries will find no difficulty in understanding why primitive people believe that mountains have souls and are presided over by gods. Something of this notion appears still to animate the souls of Icelanders, who adore their mountains and speak of them with genuine affection.

Shortly after my arrival at Reykjavík I stood before the statue of Ingólfur Arnarson, carved by the masterly hand of Iceland's greatest living sculptor, Einar Jonsson, and chatted to a young Icelandic student, who soon put to me the question that already a dozen other Icelanders had asked—what did I think of his country, and how did the mountains affect me? He talked in filial tones of Akrafjall and Esja, upon which at the time we were gazing. He had, he said, a desire to see the world, but doubted if he could ever be happy anywhere so much as in the land of his birth; a sentiment not infrequently expressed by Icelanders. This rugged, stern land seems to have a spiritual significance for its inhabitants, most of whom have more than a touch of mysticism in their make-up; many of whom believe that they have been born in it by design and not by accident. It is not a question of "my country right or wrong," but a feeling that in the scheme of things Iceland has more than a material part to play in international relations. My young acquaintance spoke for all Icelanders.

Until late at night—for here there is, during the summer, no darkness, and by the middle of June, Iceland is the land of the midnight sun—the streets are occupied by well-dressed men and women. During the daytime the centre of Reykjavík teems with them, and they are equal in personal attractiveness to any race in the world, especially the women, who are, for the main part, handsome and lovely.

There are, however, few children to be seen at this time of year, owing to the custom of the educational authorities to send them into the country during school vacation, which lasts about three months. Iceland is very "child-conscious," and takes the greatest care of its young charges. No difference is made between legitimate and illegitimate children, for undoubtedly Iceland can do with all if she is to increase her sparse population. The Armies of Occupation played, as might well be expected, a considerable part in this question. About three hundred Icelandic girls married American Service men and about fifty married British. Altogether about five hundred illegitimate children were left behind to be supported in large part by the Icelandic Government. The support of these children has cost a good deal, and the Icelandic Government intend to take the matter up with the American and British Governments with a view to re-imbursement.

When on holiday the children are housed in farmhouses in carefully selected districts and great care is taken of their health. For some unexplained reason tuberculosis was a scourge of this country and is still a grave source of concern. Gradually it is being overcome, but like leprosy it is still a danger. To me an air of quaintness pervaded the scene, owing to the admixture of the ancient and modern in a pronounced form: the younger generation have adopted almost ultra-modern clothes, in very good taste, and are as smart as Parisiens and New Yorkers at their best. But many of the older women still wear the picturesque national costume, which closely resembles that of the Norwegians, from whom it originated. Less than thirty years ago the national dress was more in evidence than today, but since the Great War, Icelanders have copied Paris rather than Bergen.

This change has not been confined to dress, but has extended to the city itself, the new parts of which differ greatly from the old. In the older stand attractive corrugated iron houses and buildings of quaint design, or of no design at all; a fashion which began about the middle of the nineteenth century. A quarter of a mile away, in the west end, around the stately Roman Catholic cathedral which stands conspicuously on an eminence, are some of the modern residences: handsome houses constructed of fortified concrete in broad thoroughfares. These residences are mainly flats, and invariably have charming gardens with pretty shrubs and flowers, for Icelanders love flowers almost to distraction. They cultivate them carefully—perhaps one should say tenderly—because flowers often find it difficult to flourish in this climate and soil. Those of us who live in warmer climes with abundant verdure can hardly imagine what Icelanders would give to have them transported in as great profusion to their land.

Reykjavík, however, is not devoid of trees, although, in common with the rest of the country, they do not attain a great height. On the whole the country around Reykjavík is very barren of flora except for dandelions, buttercups, and a few other common flowers. This must be expected of a land of volcanic rocks and largely covered with lava, much of the nourishment having been burnt out of the earth. Iceland is a plateau or tableland with only one-fourteenth. of its area lowland, and the interior of the tableland consists for the most part of barren deserts, the surface being covered by gravel, loose fragments of rocks, lava and drifts, volcanic ashes and claysoil detritus. So the experts say, and it is easy to see that they are right. Only hardy plants and annuals can hope to survive under such conditions. With the help of man there are plenty of domestic animals. But there is one notable feature about Reykjavík: it has no dogs and few cats. Dogs are forbidden in towns owing to the danger of epidemics, which on more than one occasion they are suspected of having caused. The result is the streets are not befouled by these animals, and compared with British, Icelandic towns are in this respect certainly more desirable. Dogs are confined entirely to country districts and flourish on farms.

An example of the peculiar situation arising from the smallness of the trees is seen in the public park of Reykjavík. On one side is what is meant to be a small wood, the trees of which are so stunted that anyone wishing to shut out other objects must often sit down, because to stand is to tower above them. I saw seated on the ground with an air of contentment, numbers of picnickers who appeared not to notice the smallness of the trees, and who had, to their own satisfaction, isolated themselves from the busy town just beyond, as completely as Americans seated among the Redwood trees of California!

Trees grow more freely in the northern parts of the island, where they attain their greatest height—about thirty to forty feet. The chief causes of this dearth of trees is said to have been volcanic action, which has denuded vast territories; while centuries of tree cutting to obtain fuel and the grazing of sheep in winter when the grass is covered with snow, and in the springtime when the plants are sprouting, have also played a destructive part. Replanting does not seem to have been widely attempted, although the Government is now awake to this necessity.

Dwarf willows of several varieties are common and, along with different kinds of heather and juniper, help to decorate the barrenness of the mountains and valleys and grace the gardens in the towns and villages. At one time Iceland was much more favoured, as well-marked impressions of leaves and fruit have been discovered, showing that in the tertiary period extensive forests existed. At that time the mean temperature of the country was 48° F; now it is only 35.6° F.

The day of my arrival 3rd June, had been dedicated to sailors, who have assumed the greatest importance in the country. The hotel was unable to supply mere visitors with food, as the sailors were celebrating the evening with a dinner and dance. This was the culmination of their annual appeal to the public for subscriptions for the completion and support of a Sailors' Home, in which those too old to follow their arduous and dangerous occupation can retire and spend their last days in comfort. But the Icelandic sailor is no ordinary sailor, and those that filled the dining-room and dance hall with their pretty partners were dressed as gentlemen, looking splendid in their immaculate dinner suits! The explanation is that Iceland's future lies with her fishermen, the exportation of fish having become her main industry and source of income. The trade statistics for 1943 show how important this industry is, as in that year no less than 88 per cent. of Iceland's total exports was fish! It seems incredible that any country should depend to such an extent upon this single commodity, but it is so.

Sailors are therefore held in high regard, and no one need regret being a trawler hand. At the high rate of wages presently prevailing, those following this occupation are much better able to wear evening-dress suits than those of other trades that lag so far behind. Iceland's seas have always been noted for fish, and there is no apparent diminution of the kinds that Iceland and the world wants. But the year 1943 did not reach the high water mark of fish exportation, as 1940 and 1942 both exceeded it. In 1942 fish totalled no less than 96.1 per cent of Iceland's exports.

My Icelandic friends gave me little breathing space before introducing me to the principal attractions of their country, and showed me that in at least one respect Reykjavík leads the world. It is no longer a city of coal and smoke owing to the new and magnificent system of central heating through using the natural hot water which so copiously underlies the surface of the land. These natural resources are unlimited, and there is no reason why the Reykjavík system of heating should not be extended to other towns, as, indeed, it will be in time. Reykir, the region where these thermal springs have been sunk, has more attractions than the almost boiling springs and streams and power station from whence the hot water is pumped to Reykjavík about ten miles away. It also has extensive greenhouses where the cultivation of plants and vegetables, such as tomatoes, which will not grow in the open air, is carried on. The heat used is certainly agreeable to the plants, which are notably rich in colour. Extended far enough, this use of the thermal regions should enable Iceland to cultivate even tropical plants, as, indeed, is being done, including bananas.

The utilising of thermal springs for heating greenhouses, now of such great commercial value to Iceland, appears to have been first suggested by Lady Craigie when travelling in Iceland in 1910, with her husband, Sir William Craigie. During the following winter Sir William endeavoured to get the experiment made by offering to send, free of cost, all the materials required for the building of a greenhouse at Reykhólar, but the offer was rejected.

The immense conduits which convey the hot water to the city lie exposed on the surface and gravely disfigure the countryside, but doubtless in time this defect will be remedied either by a decorative covering or by sinking them beneath the surface.

Icelanders are enthusiastic sportsmen and I had the good fortune to arrive in time to witness some pony-racing, a popular but rather rare sport. Icelandic ponies have long been world famous for their compactness, docility, strength and endurance. Before the advent of the motor car these little creatures were the only means of transportation throughout the island, and their surefootedness became proverbial. Travellers were exuberant in their praise of these pretty creatures, which are often little bigger than Shetland ponies. Although they have gone somewhat out of fashion now, they are still used, mainly in outlying districts where roads are few or non-existent, and as a rule the traveller going a long distance employs two of them, using them alternately for pack-carrying and riding. In this way forty or more miles a day can be covered, a remarkable distance considering the nature of country over which they are compelled to go. I have seen big, heavy men riding them across boulder-strewn lava beds, the little animals plodding along without making the slightest slip on what seemed to be impossible ground. Some of the old pony-tracks still remain, running alongside the motor roads which have in recent years been built through better terrain, and they speak volumes for the virtues of these ponies.

They are shaggy-haired, solemn-looking creatures, every line of their small frames indicating great strength, the rider generally looking far too big for so small a steed. They are much admired by their owners who treat them, as a rule, with the greatest tenderness. Occasionally, however, farmers, owing to poverty or lack of accommodation, leave them exposed to the elements throughout the year, including the severe winter. But so great is their hardiness that they survive this neglect and do not lessen in their docility and willingness.

Many of the inhabitants of Reykjavík keep them as pets and use them for week-end excursions, and I often met groups of Icelanders astride their steeds on their way for a day in the mountains or on a visit to their summer houses by the side of some lake or mountain.

Icelandic pony-racing is good sport, and if not up to the standard of the Derby or the Lincoln, gives no less pleasure and excitement to the public. Soon after my arrival a series of races were run under rules that would by no means have met with the approval of any but Icelanders. All races were over the same distance—300 metres—without regard to handicapping. This was a misfortune, as one of the jockeys was a little boy of ten, weighing perhaps five stone, all the others being men of from eight to twelve stone. Needless to say the boy, who was a splendid rider, won every race he rode in.

These ponies are rigorously trained by the owners for the contests but show little signs of it, as their lines differed little from the numerous other ponies used to bring their riders to the racecourse. Racing ponies are called "amblers" because of their peculiar mode of running, which consists of short quick strides without any tendency to galloping. The racecourse was extremely primitive, with a small "grand-stand" which appeared to have been hurriedly erected for the occasion. The proceedings, however, were conducted by proper officials with due pomp and dignity, the ponies being paraded upon the course long enough to enable the public to judge their efficiency and make their bets. Never more than four ponies participated in each race, and in some only three.

The course, situated on the side of a hill, had no special attractions. It had been cleared of loose stones, which literally cover large tracts around Reykjavík, the deep brown lava dust which covered the earth affording a soft footing for the ponies and an ample covering for those who overhung the improvised railing that kept the public from trespassing on the course and impeding the riders! It was great fun and everybody enjoyed themselves as much as if they had been on the finest racecourse in the world; but the primitive nature of the event clearly showed how much Icelanders have been cut off from the world and, having to find their own sources of pleasure, have found what to them seems to be an adequate representation of the "sport of kings." Now that Europe and America are practically at the door of Iceland through the airplane, it is to be hoped that pony-racing will continue, if only to keep the present pleasantly in touch with the past.

The rapid exchange of money at the pony racing was symptomatic of the extraordinary prosperity prevailing. Never in the history of Iceland has it been so well off, and up to 1940 Icelanders could not have imagined the good-fortune in store for them. Had they done so they would, undoubtedly, have welcomed the British and later the American armies of occupation more warmly. They learned in time to do this, but it was natural that at the beginning they showed resentment. Had there been no other reason for this than the objection to foreign troops forcibly landed on their shores, it would have been sufficient. No one is likely to look upon the invaders of his native land with delight; certainly not Icelanders, who have always been a liberty-loving people.

It is known that the earliest colonists left Norway to escape the tyranny of Harald the Fairhaired, who had begun subjugating the small kingdoms in that country. Many gave way, but a large number refused and were obliged to emigrate. This was the chief cause of the colonization of Iceland. Many of the present day Icelanders are descendants of some of the leading families of ancient Norway, ancestors who left their native land, taking with them their chattels and slaves. Pride of this Viking blood has never departed from the country.

An idea of the great change in their national fortune can be gauged from the fact that previous to the occupation of 1940 the average weekly income of labourers in Reykjavík was about £2 15s. 0d.; today it is about £16! The beginning of this extraordinary rise, which has been accompanied by a corresponding rise in the cost of living, was the urgent need of the British army of occupation. To induce Icelanders to help build airfields, erect huts, make roads, and perform other necessary tasks, high wages were offered, and when the American army arrived they offered still more. Since then there has taken place a steady increase which is now stabilised in a most extraordinary manner. Its economic and financial implications must be left for those who understand them; visitors from Britain and America must remain perplexed and dissatisfied. The cause is the present rate of exchange—twenty-six kronurs to the £1, with American and Canadian equivalents, making the krona cost about 9d. Actually it is worth less than 3d.

Every Britisher and American with whom I have discussed the matter, and it is a constant source of conversation, complains bitterly and inclines to the opinion that their Governments are favouring Icelanders at the expense of themselves. To the Briton it is but an extension of the misfortunes which afflict him in his native land through the coupon system and extremely high taxes. But nothing is done about it and nothing apparently will be done. I paid one krona twenty-five aurar (11¼d.) for an article that in Britain would have cost less than 1d. A hair-cut costs 3s. 9d.; an ordinary three-course lunch 9s.; a five-course dinner 16s., with most things *pro rata*. There must be some magic about international trade therefore to make it possible for the countries affected to trade with Icelanders; but that they do is shown by the abundance of goods from England and America that fill the shops. There is so much money about that most commercial salesmen need only state what they have to sell to be invited to dispose of the lot to the first customer.

One travelling salesman that I met was worried out of his life because of this, and spent two weeks trying to allocate his quota to a reasonable number of customers, all of whom seemed anxious to devour him as well as his goods. He was literally overwhelmed by Icelandic hospitality and found that he was quite unable to hold off the many kindnesses that his customers piled upon him. There is, however, nothing unusual about this. Icelanders are keen business people and will do everything within reason to ensure success; but their hospitality is not assumed merely for the occasion; it constitutes part of their conception of duty and social life.

How long this artificial condition of exchange will last it is impossible to say, but that Iceland is assured of prosperity for many years to come is evident. She is one of the few countries that have benefited by the war, and is reaping the advantages of her neutrality. Her pre-war insignificance was a guarantee of security. Having no army she was unable to defend herself; there was also the smallness of her population. While Europe starves Iceland finds fish in abundance, but still not in sufficient quantities to meet the urgent demand of hungry peoples; and judging by the way she is at present conducting her national affairs, there is little doubt that she will turn her good fortune to good account, so that no one need envy her her good fortune—perhaps not even the unfair rate of exchange.

At this time I was allowed to take only £10 out of England. The question of exchange assumes for the British visitor a very serious problem when he finds that in Iceland his pound sterling is worth only about one-third of that sum. He must expect, as I found, not the slightest sympathy or assistance from the British Consular Service, no matter how much money he may have left in Britain.

At the end of a few days, although my hospitality was assured by my sponsors, I was completely broke, and thereupon took a cheque round to the British Consul in Reykjavík, and requested him to change it. He informed me that he had no power to do so, although he was convinced that the cheque was a good one. He was absolutely adamant, and to my pleadings suggested that I ask my sponsors for some cash. When I told him that I had no wish to go cap in hand to them like a beggar, he smilingly suggested that I take it to the Icelandic Bank. This was an admission that I could get more than £10.

"Why," I asked, "should Icelanders accept a cheque which the British Government has rejected?"

The reply was the inevitable smile and a deprecating shrug of the shoulders.

After informing the Consul that I had paid very heavy taxes to receive this unsatisfactory rejection, I left the

Consulate no better off than when I had entered it. It was obvious that had I been without sponsors I could have slept on the streets so far as the British Government was concerned.

Reykjavík grows apace and the situation, not too good, is giving rise to concern among the more thoughtful Icelanders. Reykjavík has a population of between 45,000 and 48,000, recruited for the main part from country districts, where farmers are unable to retain their workers because of their inability to pay such high wages as the metropolis offers. It is commonly said that farmers are having a bad time, many of them being in a precarious state financially, and farming is the second most important industry in the country. If farming should fail and the Icelander be compelled to buy all his food abroad—he has to rely upon imports for a good deal of it—the nation's position will be bad. Icelandic country districts can hardly hope to compete with the attractions of a big city like Reykjavík, where are to be found all the amenities the modern youth seeks.

The result of this influx, which far exceeds the city's housing capacity, is peculiar. In all the outlying districts around the capital, extending for many miles, are to be found scattered houses of various types, many of them none too good. Some are pretty and attractive, but these are usually summer houses used by city dwellers only at week-ends. Indeed, these summer houses are to be found scattered also among the distant mountains and on the shores of the various lakes within a few hours' motor drive from the capital, and they are often almost inaccesible, because of the poor roads leading to them. These more distant ones are the possessions of the well-to-do who, with their powerful American motor cars, are able to negotiate almost any kind of track to the danger of the chassis.

The other houses are those erected for and by those who desire to live in or near Reykjavík. It is surprising how enterprising Icelanders are. They still possess an enormous amount of the old pioneer spirit which characterised their ancestors and those who migrate abroad today to start afresh in new and undeveloped lands. I visited one of these home-built houses and was astonished at the excellence of the job. The owner was a young electrical worker with a wife and two children. The high rents in the city had driven him out of it, and he had taken up one of the free plots of land the Government gives to those who wish to build their own homes. He had erected a large homestead made entirely of wood with the exception of the foundation, which was composed of well-laid concrete. This five-roomed house and garage had taken him, with the assistance of his two brothers—neither of whom was connected with the building trade—four or five months to make, and he intended moving in a week hence. He had drawn up his own plans, and although when I visited it the house was far from complete, it presented, under the circumstances, a good appearance. The country in which it was situated would have disheartened any Britisher used to the unemcumbered fields of England. It was covered with boulders of volcanic rock, some of them far too large to be moved by himself, for he was expected to clear the land without Government aid. The view around was all that an artist could expect if he loved the sea—rock strewn meadows and rugged mountains—but the artist would, I think, have buried his face in his hands in despair at those rocks and boulders. But not our Icelandic friend. He and his relations glowed with satisfaction at the scene, and one felt that they loved lava as much as they loved the house. Such optimism, industry and courage must be a guarantee of Iceland's future.

Every kind of shelter has been recruited to the service of the increasing population, and until more labour is found, the present condition must remain. Many families have taken up residence in the numerous Nissen Huts vacated by the British and American armies, and there are several small villages in and around Reykjavík composed entirely of these unattractive abodes. Everybody seems content, not least those who live in them; and as Icelanders are among the most hygienic people in the world, there is no danger from the point of view of sanitation.

This may be said to be the nearest Iceland today gets to igloos, and when the climate is considered one cannot refrain from smiling at the American soldiers who arrived complete with sheepskin coats to shield themselves against the icy blasts and heavy snows of what they thought to be the coldest country on earth. The truth is, Iceland is no colder than Edinburgh, and certainly, judging from my experience, has better summers. Its winters in the south are characterised by little snow, and I have just seen a photograph of a large party of visitors to Iceland, taken in the middle of last winter, standing on the harbour; not one of them is wearing an overcoat!

Shortly after my arrival I was talking to an American medical doctor who had been in Reykjavík a few weeks, and he was laughing about his own as well as his friend's misconception of the climate and country. Hearing of his appointment they had actually come to commiserate with him on his misfortune, and hoped that his sojourn in such an outlandish and undesirable spot would not last long. They too had visions of igloos and polar bears.

Ten years from now will see Reykjavík extending its environs far beyond its present built-up areas, and these unpropitious rock-bound districts will doubtless be as charming as the city itself, which at one time was no better. Among the rocks will appear lovely gardens equal in charm to those of the west-end of the Capital. The view from these areas where free grants of land are made, is on the whole even more beautiful than from the city itself, and this doubtless plays no small part in encouraging amateur house builders to try their "prentice hands." It is impossible to describe such things as the beautiful sunsets and the wonderful hues that light the sky, landscape and seascape nightly during the months of June, July and August. To observe the sun light the heavens at 2 a.m., carries with it much of the bizarre as well as of the beautiful.

3. ICELANDIC PONY

These creatures were used for all forms of transportation before the introduction of motor lorries, buses and cars

4. HEKLA

To see the waters of the bay shining with a deep blue as if it were an ocean of ink, edged by the pale green grass which lies at the foot of Esja, crowned with low-lying white clouds, is a picture not easily forgotten.

The growth of Reykjavík from the beginning of the eighteenth century, when it was a village with a population of 307, until today, has been carefully recorded in pictures. It can be compared only with colonial cities and those of the Western States of America, with this exception, that while the first dwellings there were plain log huts, Reykjavík has developed from houses the walls of which were built of rough field-stone with layers of sod between and lined inside with matchboard. The roofs were clinker-built of planks, the outside covered with greensward. The insides were of the plainest and poorest kind and one wonders how the inhabitants kept themselves warm without coal or other natural fuel. The beds were like stalls built against the walls, and when the inhabitants retired they were almost as heavily garbed as during the day-time.

The bedrooms were the living rooms, and the inhabitants slept together in the same room, irrespective of sex. So slight was the social distinction between servants and masters that they slept in the same apartment and ate in the same room, the servants and farm hands sitting, as a rule, on their beds while the farmer's family had a table in the centre of the room. Their domestic utensils were rough wooden bowls and platters, and their food of the plainest, with skyr as a mainstay. This is still a popular part of diet in both town and country, and is regarded as medicinal in its effects. It is made of milk heated to boiling point and left to cool to blood heat. Rennet is then added and allowed to stand for twenty-four hours, after which it is put through a strainer. The skyr being the white substance left in the strainer. It can be seasoned with sugar, jam, honey, or fruit juices, and eaten with milk. Skyr is very agreeable and certainly among the most nourishing of foods being particularly easy on the digestion, and I ate it as often as I could. As a rule it is eaten without coffee, a favourite beverage in Iceland, where it is made as well as anywhere else in the world. Coffee tends to curdle the skyr and inclines to create biliousness. Skyr can hardly be called a cultivated taste, as everybody that I have known who has eaten it for the first time has liked it.

After the middle of the nineteenth century wooden houses became the rule in towns and villages, but farm houses remained wedded to the old crude stone and turf style. There are still large numbers of these picturesque but none too healthy buildings scattered among the hills and plains. They seem to have been largely responsible for tuberculosis which was for so long a scourge and is still prevalent. They may also have contributed to leprosy, which has gradually yielded to science, until today there may be not more than a half-dozen cases in the land, and these are segregated in a large house just outside Reykjavík.

Concrete came into vogue in the first decades of the twentieth century, a period of great advancement in sanitation, hygiene and appearance. The roads, which were for a long time mere gravel paths, many of which still remain even in Reykjavík, have been gradually giving way to better materials, including tar macadam. Today there are all the amenities of the great cities of Europe and America, with a water supply second to none. Thus we have in Reykjavík a fine example of a modern city, in some respects ahead of other countries by virtue of its progressive engineering accomplishments.

Through its remarkable central heating system Reykjavík leads the world in this respect. From the moment Ingólfur Arnarson saw the hot steam pouring from the earth the possibilities of using this gift of nature to human advantage must have been apparent; and there is evidence that long before Snorri Sturluson, the great Icelandic historian, used it for his private open-air bath in the thirteenth century, it had been used for a similar purpose.

Hot springs about two miles from Reykjavík have been

used as a free public wash-house for generations. It is known as Thvottalaugar, *i.e.*, "washing springs," and these same waters were used for centrally heating houses as early as 1930, the water being pumped by a small motor—about seventy houses being supplied.

The results were so satisfactory that it was decided to carry the scheme to its logical conclusion and centrally heat the whole of the Capital.

The work was begun in 1939; boring being made at South Reykir, about twelve miles north of Reykjavík, drillings averaging a depth of 340 metres, the deepest being 750. This meant drilling through solid rock—basalt, dolerite, sandstone and conglomerate.

When the war broke out operations had to be suspended owing to the inability to procure efficient engineers and materials from abroad, most of which came from Denmark and the United States. The work was eventually resumed by Danish engineers and the first house from the new plant was supplied on 1st December, 1943. Today more than three thousand houses, or 90 per cent. of Reykjavík, are heated, and the number grows constantly; soon every house will be supplied. The heat of the water at its source is 86° centigrade, and in the town 80° centigrade. It is not much used in industry and is not likely to be for some time as the authorities have decided to concentrate on houses and public buildings, and for the time being the pressure of water is not sufficiently great.

Because of this the work is being extended and in addition to the fourteen deep wells at South Reykir, new wells are to be sunk at Nordur Reykir, about two miles further on. The pressure enables 300 litres per second to pass through culverts which contain two pipe lines each, of fourteen inches diameter, surrounded by a layer of turf, ample air space and then the concrete covering. The water is alkaline.

The advantages have, of course, been considerable, for in addition to saving fuel, which had to be imported from abroad at great expense, the town is cleaner, whilst convenience and health derived from constant hot water is incalculable. Other towns have been keen to follow this example and Akureyri, Húsavík and Hafnarfjördur are all drilling for water, in each case well out of the town. At Húsavík hot water has been found under the sea, but this makes no difference to its quality.

The whole cost of the undertaking to Reykjavík municipality, for it is a local and not a national enterprise, has been about £400,000, with an annual return of about £80,000, so that from a financial point of view the scheme has proved eminently successful.

The manner in which the supply is made to the houses is simple. The water is first pumped into a number of huge tanks on a hill on the outskirts of the city, and then run through the forty kilometres of street mains. The water is then run through the house connections and sold through a meter at approximately 3¼d. per cubic metre from 15th October to the 15th May, and thereafter at half price.

From the beginning special attention was paid to heating schools and other public institutions; the water in the schools, after passing through the radiators being used for baths. At present two public swimming baths are supplied, and others are to be built.

CHAPTER 3

ICELAND AND ICELANDERS

WHY do Icelanders favour concrete dwellings? No matter how much one may praise the artistic and utilitarian results Reykjavík builders have attained, the fact remains that brick houses look better; there is something hard and cold about concrete which appears to reserve it almost exclusively, viewed from an aesthetic standpoint, for large commercial buildings, dams and walls. Concrete doubtless has many points over corrugated iron in house construction, for corrugated iron has the outstanding defect of looking cheap. By comparison, therefore, the modern Icelandic concrete buildings are an improvement on the older method. But why not use brick?

The answer is that bricks would have to be imported at great expense because Iceland has no means of making them herself. True, some of the ingredients of concrete also have to come from abroad, but some can be supplied on the spot and that makes for convenience and economy. But the chief factor favouring the use of this material is that it is very suitable for the climate, keeps out fog and cold, and stands firm against earthquake shocks. Not that Reykjavík has had many of these unpleasant experiences, although she has had sufficient to make the inhabitants conscious of what might happen. A year or two ago Reykjavík, I heard, was disturbed by an explosion followed immediately by a tremor that ceased almost as soon as it began. No damage was done, but had it been a little more violent some of the weaker buildings might have collapsed, but not the concrete ones.

Iceland appears to be a seething cauldron which finds an outlet for its pent-up forces through numerous natural ventholes scattered all over the country. Reykjavík derived its name partly from this fact; freely translated Reykjavík means "Steam Bay." Iceland seems to be a very dangerous place, and needs to be visited to have this impression removed. It is not encouraging to read that Iceland is one of the most volcanic areas of the world; and that volcanic action has been going on continuously since tertiary times. Quite recently Heckla has again become active. History is not too encouraging either, as during historic times there have been eruptions from no less than twenty-five vents. 107 volcanoes are known to exist, with thousands of craters, large and small, and the lava streams which have flowed from them cover an area of 4,650 square miles.

Viewed from this angle alone Icelanders may, indeed, be regarded as an intrepid race. They certainly show no signs of anxiety on this subject. But for all that, nature has not been altogether kind to them. When she blows up in Iceland she does so with a will. After the eruption of 1625, ashes were carried as far as Bergen, Norway. In 1875 a rain of ashes fell on the west coast of Norway from an eruption in Iceland, and took less than twelve hours to do the journey. It would not have given great cause for complaint if nothing worse than the transportation of ashes alone had been involved, but, alas, much destruction at home has always been done by these upheavals. One has only to gaze upon the vast areas of contorted lava to see how much damage volcanoes can do, and how persistent is the ill effect.

Lava seems to be good for nothing except making roads, and these are quite good. It is only lately that the Government has seriously turned this feature to use. Lava has the very heart burned out of it before it cools, and is almost good for nothing. But, alas, lava when freshly cast forth from the bowels of the earth is hot and consumes anything it can, and through that, hunger and disease have from time to time followed in the wake of eruptions. Take the worst instance on record: from Laki at Skapta, in 1783, came the largest volume of lava known in Iceland, covering an area of 218 square miles. It destroyed so much pasture that animals died of disease and hunger. 11,500 cattle, 28,000 horses and 190,000 sheep succumbed. After this came famine and 9,500 people, or one-fifth of the population died. The truth is, earthquakes are frequent but not harmful as a rule; but the one in 1896 destroyed 161 farms and damaged 155 others, in a population of about 80,000 people.

Concrete houses reinforced with steel rods are therefore not a bad idea. Furthermore, concrete is not friable and Iceland finds house building so expensive that she needs must build for duration. I saw a house in the outskirts of Reykjavík containing about eighteen rooms, a very large house for this town. It stood in about half an acre of cultivated garden and looked severely attractive. At the outside it would have sold in England for £5,000 at present war prices; in Reykjavík it would sell for about £10,000! A house being built, composed of two small flats each containing four smallish rooms is costing 125,000 krona.

Volcanic smoke and lava do not issue only from craters. Many fissures afford the same phenomenon. While upon the subject of volcanoes it may be as well to mention Askja, the largest in Iceland. Its crater alone is 34 square miles in area!

This reference to earthquakes and volcanoes may cast anything but a good aura upon this remarkable island, and warn the timid off; but there is no need to be nervous. Human astuteness has discovered the reliable places in which to live; and it is a reliable guess to say that one is safer in Iceland than in Britain, France or Germany, which, being free from earthquakes, find a substitute in war with its air-raids, guns and atomic bombs. Iceland is, in fact, much safer.

Man is naturally influenced by his environment. Just as sunny Cuba makes its impecunious population happy and contented, and sunny California keeps its somewhat elderly, opulent inhabitants buoyant and cheerful, so the thermal nature of Iceland reacts upon its people. One cannot live close to danger and not be affected by it.

All around one can see what in olden times the inhabitants believed to be visible proof of the existence of hell, in the boiling pools, geysers and hot springs. As one passes through the mountains, every now and then clouds of vapour appear belching from the hillside or in the valleys. To the ignorant this must have been bewildering and nerve-racking, for with all their intelligence, the early settlers knew nothing of science; certainly nothing of modern science. In the presence of a mystery one guess may be as good as another, and these superstitious men and women, with their firm belief in nature gods, must have felt that in this new, strange and awe-inspiring land mysterious forces were at work that must either be placated or worshipped. No doubt this was the chief reason why Christianity was not adopted until the year 1000 A.D., and then by compromise.

The old Viking faith remained so strong that the influence of the Irish monks who came to the island nearly a century before Ingólfur Arnarson have had no effect; they fled the country immediately upon the arrival of the Norsemen. The compromise was arranged by an old pagan who was requested to adjudicate, and after careful consideration he ruled that Christianity should be the public faith, but that anyone could, if he wished, worship in the old faith in private. His idea was to establish peace among a warlike people who were very susceptible to religious influence. War meant disunity, and that, in its turn, spelt national weakness. Björn Thórdarson in his book "Iceland Past and Present" says: "The people are still to some extent of a two-fold faith. It believes that it still may be guided by the family spirit of its heathen ancestors . . . On the other hand it believes that God will help it if it helps itself."

It is not difficult to see that Icelanders have strong within them a tendency to nature worship, which may be more than a mere "hang-over" from those early Norwegians who gazed in nervous admiration at the first geyser and boiling pool. They seem never to cease admiring the mountains and valleys, and will even grow ecstatic over a lava field. Where others see nothing but bareness and useless territory, an Icelander will see beauty and power. They are a nation of artists and poets, singing songs about their landscape and seascape and seeing grace and loveliness in scattered boulders, and in the fantastic shapes. With natural optimism they see the promise of God in a volcano and gaping crevasse, and feel assured that Iceland is destined to play an important part in the scheme of things.

There is nothing insincere about all this; it is part of their psychological make-up with an emotional content which has been formed throughout the eleven centuries since they first occupied the land. Their present aim is to acquaint others with these natural wonders, and they feel confident that if they succeed their present population may be swelled to at least a million! They know, they say, that the country can support them, and that it needs them.

It could be done, as there is plenty of space and arable land. In an area of 40,437 square miles and a coast line of 3,730 miles there is a good deal of fine country lying round the borders and in the valleys. It is computed that although only one-fourteenth of the island is habitable to any extent, this would be sufficient for their purpose. There is plenty of uncultivated land which could be turned into excellent farms, which with modern methods of cultivation could revolutionise the country. Within a few miles of Reykjavík large areas lie fallow, and Halldora Sigurjonson, an Icelandic-Canadian farmer with whom I travelled about the island looking for arable land was indignant at the neglect, and concluded that the people were lazy. All it needed, she said, was a plough and good farming. Much of her criticism referred to plateau as well as low lands.

The mystical traits of the Icelanders has given rise to an extensive and fascinating folk-lore and there are a large number of people who claim to have had supernormal experiences. Some of their stories are very impressive and would please any psychical researcher or believer in communications with the dead. A few years ago an immense amount of interest was aroused throughout the the country through a strange event which showed that two boys who had been accidentally pushed into the sea, communicated the fact almost at once to a group of people sitting together a great way off. These people could not have known of the accident by normal means, and it was concluded that the news of the tragedy had actually been communicated by the spirits of the drowned children.

Notwithstanding their inclination to mysticism Icelanders cannot be called a very religious people, especially the younger generation. They have a State Church with a well-educated clergy; but the clergy assume no special costume when not performing their priestly duties. No country can be less creed-bound or more tolerant, and the effect is agreeable. Everybody is made more friendly by the national teaching that everyone is entitled to his own belief, and very little proselytising is indulged in. The service that I attended in the Cathedral was picturesque and dignified; and although I could not understand one word the pastor said, it was obvious that the congregation listened with wrapt attention. My surprise was great when I learned that the subject of the sermon was to show that phenomena known to psychical researchers and Spiritualists were paralleled in the Bible, and that the preacher was President of the Icelandic Society for Psychical Research.

A few days later I had the pleasure of having tea with Bishop Sigurgeir Sigurdsson, Primate of Iceland, and from his conversation found that he was as much interested in other people's beliefs as in his own. With him too the scientific spirit predominated, and he believed that nothing but good could come from science being able to prove that man survives death.

Every clergyman that I have met here has held the same point of view, not because they necessarily believe that such evidence has been produced, but because of the way they view life. Their interests extended beyond the limits of their own small island to the world in general. They kept in close touch with international affairs, not merely to criticise but also to learn. This must be one of the blessings that small communities bestow upon themselves. There is practically no class distinction in Iceland, the rights of man being upheld even more meticulously than in the United States, which so proudly boasts of its famous Constitution. This may be one of the reasons why America influences Iceland so much. The younger generation have adopted many American phrases and the American modes to a large extent. Both are republics, both believe sincerely in the equal rights of all men, and both offer opportunities for every citizen to rise to the highest position in the State—the Presidency. There are no titles in Iceland and this as much as anything makes social relations among the people more pleasant.

The original seat of their freedom is Thingvellir, about 30 miles from Reykjavík, where the first parliament in the world was held in 930 A.D. The spot is sacred to every Icelander and no one is, if possible, allowed to leave the country without visiting it.

My Icelandic friends took me there a few hours after I had set foot on shore, and it will be impossible to forget that interesting drive. Along that same route must have travelled some of the people who met to elect their first parliament. There had been no hurry about it, every care being taken not only to find the most convenient spot at which to hold the Althing, since members and their followers would have to meet there annually. For much less than one hundred years after the first settlement of the island there was no central government, each leader of a group of settlers having to decide matters as they arose, and maintain law and order within the bounds over which his rule extended. Before long some of the more powerful men established assemblies with legislative and judicial powers. Sometimes several of them combined to form a common assembly. Thus for some time the settlement went on in a loose way.

It was impossible for this to continue indefinitely and it grew more and more essential that the people should recognise the same laws and principles of justice. This was particularly necessary in case of invasion, for it was known that King Harald of Norway was desirous of ruling the island, thus re-establishing the very conditions that had driven the early settlers to seek a new home. There arose, in time, the question of framing a code of laws, no easy matter for a people who, for so long, had been separated from Europe. Úlfljót, a member of a distinguished family, undertook the task, and went to Norway and perhaps some other countries, with a view of studying the best way to form a suitable constitution. He returned to Iceland in 927, after an absence of three years, with his projected code.

After another three years spent in serious consideration of Úlfljót's suggestions, a general place of assembly was sought, one that would easily be accessible from all parts of the island. Úlfljót's code was accepted, and the first Icelandic republic established. The land became a free and independent state. Thirty-six (later thirty-nine) local divisions, each represented by a leading man of the district, bearing the name of "Gothi", combined to form the new state, and the functions of government were placed upon a sound footing. The Althing was thus formed and Iceland became in very truth the "Mother of Parliaments."

The results were salutary. All freemen had the same rights, and very soon serfdom ceased. Judges were appointed who personally exercised legislative functions at the Althing.

According to Icelanders, Thingvellir (the Plain of the Parliament) is second to none in the whole country for beauty and for convenience. The view is extremely picturesque and situated on a plain between two immense rifts, the sides of which are some three miles apart.

CHAPTER 4

THINGVELLIR

NOBODY should write about Thingvellir without first visiting it more than once. It is impossible otherwise to understand why Icelanders revere it so much and speak of it so proudly and affectionately. Thingvellir is to them much more than an historical place. In addition to tradition it has an atmosphere all its own. My first impression on seeing it was that it merely possessed great scenic beauty and charm. Its form and setting are certainly unique; but closer acquaintance made me realise that it was much more.

The approach from Reykjavík, which lies to the west, is extraordinarily attractive. Just before entering Almannagjá, the weird gorge which leads to the plain below, one should stand awhile on the edge of the plateau overlooking Thingvellir, and see with what a masterly hand Nature has carved out this extraordinary scene. Thingvellir is a combination of rural beauty, strange rising uplands and rugged fierce volcanic structures, edged on three sides by lofty mountains and on the fourth by a magnificent lake. It is a breath-taking scene. One feels that it would have been a serious misfortune if those old law-makers had decided to meet elsewhere. This extensive natural picture bears all the deep threatening colours that characterise most of Iceland's austere landscapes, for Iceland is a threatening as well as an appealing country.

I have visited nearly thirty countries, ranging from the borders of the arctic circle to those of the antarctic; have seen the luscious verdure of tropical and semi-tropical climes; gazed with admiration at the wonderful beauties of the Blue Mountains of New South Wales; viewed the sharp-peaked Alps of New Zealand and the mighty Rockies of the U.S.A. and Canada; marvelled at the parsimoniousness of Nature as I gazed across the arid deserts of Arabia; yet only one place has filled me with greater emotion and awe than Thingvellir, and that was the Grand Canyon of Colorado. Thingvellir, one feels, must still be the resort of the shades of those early settlers who derived their origin from Viking ancestry, and who first met here to rule the people of this strange fire-eaten land.

For nine centuries Thingvellir was the heart of the public life of Iceland. Here the national assembly, the Althing, gathered annually from the very inception of the Icelandic Republic in 930, and continued in some form or other until 1798. Here too the earlier outstanding events of Iceland's history took place, the leading men of the nation meeting every summer to deal with problems of the day. During the greater part of the life of this small scattered nation, Thingvellir has been the Mecca of all Iceland's sons and daughters.

The first Althing was far from being a pure democracy. In those far off days no nation had any such meaning for that word. The first Icelandic constitutional government was in effect an aristocratic oligarchy. For many centuries the members of the legislature were recruited from the leading families of Iceland, and not until recent times has anything approaching true democracy been established. It was, however, far removed from any form of dictatorship, and at no time have Icelanders regarded any member of their race as worthy of the name of king. Today, having separated from Denmark, it is again a republic, as democratic as any state in the world.

About the time when most of the settlers, or land-takers as the Icelanders term them, had established themselves, which was roughly half a century after the first settler arrived, they decided to hold a central assembly annually. In the sagas it is recorded that two foster-brothers, or "sworn brothers," named Úlfljótur and Grímur geitskór, were mainly responsible for this. Úlfljótur prepared the first code of laws and Grímur geitskór chose the site on which the assembly was to be held. He chose it because of its favourable position, as it is said to be situated comparatively near the centre of the country; and even if this be not strictly true, it is certainly most accessible. Furthermore, it borders on one of the largest stretches of lowlands, and has all the advantages requisite for holding a large assembly. There is, for instance, a spacious plain on which people may gather, plenty of excellent drinking water, and ample pasture for the numerous ponies of those who attended. The birch-wood to the east of the plain furnished an ample supply of firewood for cooking food and brewing ale, while the lake—the largest in the country—was well stocked with fish, both char and trout. As the neighbouring districts were inhabited, a plentiful supply of food was assured, and nothing was overlooked. If the scenic beauty of the place appealed to these foster-brothers, they certainly must have felt satisfied with their choice.

Besides being a legislative assembly the Althing possessed judicial powers, and near the eastern wall of the Almannagjá can still be seen the natural judgment seat from which judicial sentences were promulgated. The site was well chosen, as it enabled the judges to address the assembled host standing in full view just below them on the plain, their voices being thrown back by the huge wall of lava behind the little plateau on which they sat. From this point—the Hill of Laws—the view of Thingvellir is extensive and the law-makers were able, as they dispensed justice, to see every part of the plain.

The Althing consisted of 147 members who sat on benches in the open air when the weather permitted, and after the year 1000, when the weather was unpropitious, they retired to the Church built by King Ólafur Haraldsson of Norway a few years after the Althing had legalised Christianity. The exact spot in the open air at which the legislative body met is not known, but it is believed to be east of the little river, Oxara.

One thing, however, is certain, that on the larger of these islets contestants who could not settle their disputes legally, resorted to the right of private combat and fought to the death. This manner of settling disputes was, however, made illegal a few years after the introduction of Christianity.

They were a hardy, high-spirited people, often driven by the awkwardness of their situation to drastic methods, and they resorted frequently to the death penalty, not because they wished to destroy so much as because they had no means of finding safe custody for lawbreakers. But, it is said, although some authorities regard the whole claim as fictitious, they did not always deny the prisoner a chance to escape; in some instances giving him the opportunity to go free by leaping across a dangerous chasm, failure causing him to fall into the waters below and drown. The chance was admittedly slight, and it is recorded that only one man ever succeeded.

To ramble among these interesting sights, imagining the conditions prevailing in those earlier days of the Althing, is to conjure up romantic pictures in which fierce but not always uncouth men and women met to relax from their arduous toil, to debate, legislate and play. The plain through those eventful two weeks each year must have presented an animated scene, in which the younger members of the gathering, leaving the more serious business to their elders, played games, particularly practising wrestling, which is still one of the most popular of sports among Icelanders. Records show that other forms of entertainment were indulged in, and among pleasant stories that have been handed down, are some which tell of friendships knit and compacts made between both young and old. Here, too, attended tanners, sword cutlers, brewers and beggars, each adding something attractive to the stirring scene.

At the foot of the Hill of Laws can still be seen the remains of the foundations of the "budir," or booths, in which the more important personages resided during the session. Some lived in tents, and the sagas say that both they and the more substantial budir existed on both sides of the river. The booths were usually made of stone, timber and turf, with tent-roofs draped inside with fabric made of Icelandic homespun.

Similar buildings are still to be seen in the more remote districts, but with more substantial roofs. These booths were small and unpretentious, as became a race who had not yet succeeded in conquering the natural forces against which their strength was constantly pitted.

Because the early dwellings had been constructed of uncemented stone and turf, it is not surprising that Iceland is singularly devoid of ancient edifices and their relics. Buildings thus constructed are not likely to last long nor to leave much evidence of their existence behind. These foundations of the budir are good examples of the general situation, although it is only the budir of later date that have left remains, though from an antiquarian point of view, they are unimpressive. They consist of little more than turf outlines of the foundations. The Government and private organisations are now fully alive to the necessity of finding and preserving these ancient memorials, and in some districts I saw the results of private efforts in this direction.

There was much to inspire and interest the visitor in the way of natural wonders, ranging from deep chasms in the lava beds, dangerous crevices, and the lovely waters of crystal streams flowing from the distant mountains. Beautiful waterfalls may be regarded as part of the natural scenery of this rock-bound land; and Thingvellir has been specially favoured by Öxaráfoss, which falls sheer from high cliffs and rushes away in a miniature cataract. The very hills that one must climb to reach the elevated position from which so many wish to see Öxaráfoss are full of natural beauty. Crude in their lava setting, one finds life striving valiantly to live, and thereby adding charm to the aridness; for scattered among the rocks are to be seen lovely little golden, pink, red and white flowers, some growing out of small patches of heather. None find much nourishment, and so grow only a few inches in height, but all contributing enchantment to the captivating scene; especially when, every now and then, a solitary long-legged bird, about the size of a sea-gull, settles on rock or boulder, uttering its unusual single-note call.

No wonder Icelanders love poetry so well that even at their public gatherings, as on National Day, in open air auditoriums, elocutionists read and recite to the assembled crowds poems from the works of popular poets. Thingvellir called to my mind some lines of Gudmundur Magnusson's poem, *Dreamland*:—

O, come with me to my land,
With moor and heathered highland
And summer sweet and long—
A beauteous inland island
Alive with scent and song.
No other place appeased me,
Each pretty charm that seized me
With tender mem'ries teems,
It's all that ever pleased me.
It is my land of dreams.

It is only to be expected that a country which is believed to be shared with elves, brownies, water beings, dwarfs and wraiths, should have its lucky and unlucky places. That one should pay due homage to these mysterious forces if one would ward off danger and induce gain from them, such as good health and good fortune, goes without saying. Thingvellir would indeed be lacking in its full measure of appeal if it were devoid of such things.

Gjá Gorge, or "Money Gorge," meets this requirement. No one need go to Thingvellir and come away without at least a hope, which, if not fulfilled, will have afforded pleasure. All that one has to do is lean over the pretty bridge which marks this spot, and throw an unwanted coin into the pellucid waters that run beneath. For so small an investment one may depart with a glow of anticipation that the water god may return the investment manifold. One glance into the gorge will suffice to convince the most sceptical that superstition still glows warmly in the human breast. The waters of this enchanted stream literally sparkle with thousands of coins which lie in all directions on the sides and bottom. "This," said one Icelander to me, "is the real Bank or Iceland." Well, doubtless all the deposits have been small, but contributed from almost every country in the world; and even if the returns are not guaranteed no one who has subscribed has gone away entirely unrewarded. A veritable fortune lies revealed, and valiant attempts have been made to redeem it; but the waters of the gorge have always proved to be too cold for those who have plunged into it in an attempt to reach the coins.

On first acquaintance, Thingvellir is liable to give the impression of being a kind of fairyland, where goblins dwell. But a more intimate association causes to grow upon the mind the feeling of some mighty power slumbering beneath its remarkable charm; a power that at some time or other shook the country and turned it over. This convulsion left rugged wounds which form grotesque configurations about three miles apart. The very air here is deceitful, making objects appear much nearer than they really are. The western ridge, Almannagjá, is indescribably rugged, and when passing through the gorge of which it forms the sides, it is impossible not to feel that nature must have been hurt by the terrible rent which tore her body asunder. Hrafnagjá, the eastern wall, is less imposing, but from a geological and seismical point of view not less interesting.

I have never passed through either gorge without being thrilled. Larger, more imposing gorges do exist but none more bizarre and enchanting. The lava rocks of Almannagjá have taken full advantage of their fire nature and assumed a hundred grotesque forms. It requires very little imagination to agree with romantic Icelanders that, as the sun sweeps the tops of these harshly-ripped eminences Vikings may be seen stalking majestically along. Or better still, as the dimmer rays of the evening fall upon them, especially when the moon plays a part, there may be seen a Viking ship in full sail with the oarsmen straining to propel it through tempestuous waters.

Half the art of seeing Thingvellir is to become a painter, a poet and a sculptor. To insist on seeing it in a prosaic light or merely as a tourist anxious for a brief distraction, is desecration. Thingvellir is not of today only; it is of all time. Lying exposed on its bosom, for those who have eyes to see and souls to feel, are some of the greatest and gravest moments in the history of a remarkable people.

The first republic of Iceland came to an end in 1264. Then the laws of the country underwent a change and with them the nature of the national assembly. It lost its power and significance as a legislative body and became mainly judicative. In 1798 the Althing was removed from Thingvellir to Reykjavík, and two years later it was abolished. It was not revived until more than forty years afterwards, and then in changed form. Here its history belongs to another chapter. But Thingvellir was deep in the heart of every Icelander and could never be forgotten and the nation has often held special assemblies there, particularly when matters of very grave importance arose. It was as if the legislators felt that in Thingvellir they could consult the shades of their ancestors and from them receive wise guidance. The Icelander has always been something of an ancestor worshipper. Here, too, in 1874, was celebrated the millenial anniversary of the first settlers; and there are those who believe it ought still to be the place where the Althing holds its sessions.

CHAPTER 5

JÓN SIGURDSSON

BY a stroke of good luck I was in Reykjavík on Victory Day and also a few days later on Iceland's National Day, 17th June. Sir Gerald Shepherd, the popular British Minister and his wife, sent out invitations to British subjects in Reykjavík to meet at his Residence. These invitations included those who had, by marriage, adopted Icelandic nationality.

Among the company were a number of British airmen who had just arrived at Reykjavík to render assistance, if required, to some Canadian airmen who were crossing the Atlantic from the Dominion. Memory must, on this occasion, have sat heavily upon most of these young men, judging by the number of ribbons that decorated their tunics.

The most excited of a rather quiet and sedate crowd were two or three British women who had married Icelandic husbands. These ladies were evidently proud of the land of their adoption, and certainly spoke highly of Icelanders as a whole. It had fallen to them to uphold the prestige of Britain when, at the beginning of the Occupation, Icelanders looked upon our troops as unwelcome invaders.

There were no speeches during the Victory Celebrations, and after an hour or two of quiet conversation the company drifted out as inconspicuously as it had drifted in.

Iceland's National Day was a much more exciting event and held to commemorate their independence and the birth of Jón Sigurdsson, the national hero who fought so effectively for the social and political freedom of his fellow countrymen. He is regarded as "Iceland's favourite son."

The entire population of Reykjavík, and many visitors from all over the island, filled Austurvöllur, the central square of the capital, to overflowing, the festivities continuing until the following day; not difficult, since there is no night at this period of the year.

Icelanders know how to enjoy themselves in a quiet restrained way. There were one or two unusual features about the long procession that marched from the University to Austurvöllur, where stand the House of Parliament and the Cathedral. In strict keeping with their admiration for Swedish drill and pattern marches, the students paraded round the square in the centre of which stands a statue of Jón Sigurdsson.

Although Iceland has no military flags it has a national flag, and this, with numerous banners belonging to various arts, crafts, guilds and benefit societies, was very much in evidence.

Icelandic processions celebrating national events are unlike those of other countries, because there are no military displays. Their place is taken by male and female athletes, who look extremely attractive in their neat costumes devised to show to the best advantage the splendid physique of the wearers. The sight is quite refreshing to those accustomed to the pomp and ceremony of militant nations.

After the demonstrators reached their respective stations in the pretty garden in the centre of the square, holding their banners aloft, there was a stir as the President and Prime Minister advanced from the House of Parliament to place the wreath before the statue of Jón Sigurdsson.

Every country has its national heroes, and whilst much is heard about Napoleon, George Washington and Frederick the Great, it is doubtful if the name of Jón Sigurdsson has extended far beyond the shores of his native land. Yet he was a truly great man who would have stood out conspicuously had he belonged to any other country.

Owing largely to his work, Iceland today grapples with international problems in much the same manner as Britain and the United States of America. In other words, he helped more than any other single person to make Iceland a country and not merely a dependency.

If Jón Sigurdsson is viewed in this broad way, his greatness becomes apparent, and the remarkable service that he rendered to the freedom of his people fully appreciated.

The spirit that animated him may be compared with that which animated Garibaldi and Simon Bolivar, although, unlike them, he did not resort to force of arms.

Running through his veins was the blood of famous Icelandic forebears, including Snorri Sturluson the historian, and the equally celebrated Bishop Jón Arason of Holar. The son of a country parson, Jón Sigurdsson grew up on his father's farm and took his share in the ordinary work of an Icelandic farm hand. It was, and still is, common for Icelandic clergymen to combine farming with their priestly functions. The work of a farm hand in Iceland was perhaps much more arduous than in any other country, owing to the ungracious nature of the soil, and the poverty which generally prevailed in the early part of the nineteenth century. Jón Sigurdsson was born 17th June, 1811, and died 7th December, 1879, and therefore lived through a period which, if transitory in the mode of cultivation prevailing on Icelandic farms, was still crude when he died. In this way Jón was brought into intimate touch with the lives of the poorest peasants, and through that grew to regard them in some respect as his special charge. They certainly remained, along with the clergy, his most ardent supporters throughout his political career. His young life was therefore spent in close touch with the greater part of the national life of his country at a time when it had no representative government.

He was twenty-nine years old before the Royal decree was issued promising that a representative government should be established in Iceland, which had been under Danish rule since 1380. From that date the royal power had increased from time to time, until, at the time of Jón Sigurdsson's birth, Iceland was in complete subjection to Denmark. It was at this stage of his country's history that

Jón Sigurdsson began to show his great foresight, wisdom and determination. At the time of the royal decree, 1840, it was suggested that the new parliament should be called by the name of the older assemblies, Althing, and meet at Thingvellir.

There was doubtless no ill intention on the part of Denmark in making this proposal, but rather a desire to please Icelanders; it also arose from the realisation that the assembly would not be an independent body and do little more than placate the Icelandic people.

This was a pretty shrewd move, as there can be no doubt that the Icelander of 1840 was not less enamoured of Thingvellir and the Althing of ancient days than he is today; and had the proposition been passed, it is evident that the new representative body modelled on old lines, would have been little more than a cipher. A sop that would have calmed the troubled minds of the more progressive elements, and lulled Iceland to sleep once more.

Jón Sigurdsson vigorously opposed Thingvellir as the seat and insisted that patriotic sentiment should be abandoned in favour of prudence and commonsense. Time has shown how wise he was in insisting that Reykjavík was the logical place for the Althing to meet. At this time Reykjavík consisted of little more than a number of scattered farms, built in the old style of stone and turf, surrounded by crude stone walls and a windmill; but already it was showing signs of becoming an important town. It had a large church and one or two buildings which might well be classed as imposing in those days. Ships were appearing more frequently in the bay, and the prospects were sufficiently promising for Sigurdsson to realise that with its natural advantages Reykjavík would, in time, become the chief commercial centre of Iceland. The success of his proposal to make Reykjavík the seat of Government naturally resulted in stimulating the rapid growth of the town, which twenty-five years later had become worthy of the name of city, small though it was.

Jón saw that Reykjavík would develop under his proposed political influence not only as the seat of government, but also as the cultural and historic centre. His reward was that at the first election of the new Althing he was elected for the county of Isafiord, which he continued to represent until his death. It is surprising to find that at the time of these keen activities he was residing, not in Iceland, but in Copenhagen, whither in his youth he had gone to the University, and had remained. Copenhagen afforded him much more scope for his genius. At no time was he freed from the urgent necessity of earning his own livelihood.

From the very first it became clear that he was endowed with all the qualities essential to a great leader of the people; and to his splendid mental qualities he added a "stately and chivalrous appearance."

His election to the Althing necessitated his returning to Iceland every two years to take his seat in parliament. Although he was only thirty-four years old when first elected it was evident that he was the best mind in the assembly, and his resolute speaking helped to create a courageous spirit among his fellow members, while his clear thinking soon caused them to look to him for guidance. It is said by those who knew him intimately, that he could form a clear opinion on every subject which he considered of importance, and never, even in the darkest days, despaired of the ultimate victory of his cause. To clear thinking he added a second virtue which undoubtedly ensured his success, a strength or quality well expressed in the motto that he made for himself: "Never give way." Such a drastic motto could never have been justified except by one who not only felt that his judgments were sound, but knew they were. This feature is characteristic of this extraordinary man.

His aims were so comprehensive that they embraced everything necessary to the success of his country. In the whole of the land, he appears to have been the one person by nature endowed to lead it from its mental as well as its political and commercial bondage. It must remain a mystery how the Icelanders, a race naturally vigorous mentally as well as physically, and with what one would suppose to be an inborn love of freedom, could have become so lost to a sense of their rights and privileges, as they were at this time. This deplorable state of affairs is shown by the apathy of the masses when Sigurdsson made his first endeavours, and by the opposition that he met from the more prosperous members of an impoverished people, who, rather than endanger their personal comfort, were prepared to put up with the gravest inconveniences imposed upon them by the Danes.

The explanation must be sought in the fact that the despotism had been so long that they had become used to their chains and had grown to like them. For about two centuries before Jón Sigurdsson began his work, Iceland had become impoverished through Danish exactions, bad seasons and ignorance; all of which had given rise to a deadly apathy from which sprang fear lest matters became worse.

The national spirit was almost extinct. The evil results of the iron hand with which they had been ruled is to be seen today in the aversion shown by Icelanders towards Denmark. It may be compared with that of Eire towards England. Trade had been wilfully restricted by the Danes for about two and a half centuries, inflicting grave misfortunes on the country. At one time there had been a strict commercial monopoly, but this was abolished in 1787, and freedom of trade somewhat extended; but trade continued to be encumbered by many restrictions.

None but Danish subjects were allowed to trade there, except on terms so exhorbitant that competition was practically eliminated. All merchandise, both domestic and foreign, had first to go to Denmark in order that that country should profit by it. This was not only an intolerable nuisance, but also a grave injustice, almost banning foreign trade, owing to the excessive freightage involved.

Of that period we read: "Nothing led to the decay of trade in Iceland so much as the king usurping the whole of the trade of the island, and affixing certain prices to the whole of the produce. No one dared to sell anything except to royal factors, nor to them at a price above that stated in a printed list circulated throughout the country. This monopoly at first produced considerable revenue for the royal treasury, but people were impoverished by it. The royal factors then began to oppress the natives and rob their own master, so that at last the profits were less than the expense. The Danish Government therefore issued proclamations declaring the commerce of the island free; but did nothing more than sell royal privileges to a body of merchants, who enjoyed under certain stipulations, the exclusive right to trade with the island. The natives were under the same restrictions as before. No ships except the company's could enter Icelandic ports to traffic. So rigidly was the law applied that as many as twenty strokes with the cat-o'-nine-tails were inflicted on one man for selling two fish beyond the area allotted to him.

Jón Sigurdsson wrote vigorously against these iniquities, pleading for free trade. His views were not only opposed by the Danish Government, but also by many of his fellow countrymen who had been reared on the assumption that it was Denmark alone who supplied Iceland with what scanty means she possessed. This opposition naturally disappointed Jón, but he was broadminded enough to recognise the effect of education, environment, and custom. He tolerantly admitted that his opponents were not animated by evil motives, but merely misunderstood the situation. The restrictions, he held, had been imposed so long that obedience to them had become a habit.

Fortunately the spirit of 1848 which was animating a large part of Europe, extended to Iceland, and there were indications, soon after the election of the first of the new Althing, that Iceland was becoming politically conscious.

The extraordinary nature of Sigurdsson's mind is amply shown in the tolerant spirit and patience with which he viewed his timid and reactionary fellow-countrymen.

Not for one moment does he appear to have lost his temper, but with clear insight saw the causes of their conduct, although they were hidden from themselves. He will go down in history as one of the most kindly and patient politicians of all time, and this characteristic contributed very largely to his ultimate success.

His policy was similar to that which led the British Parliament to agree to dominion status for some of its larger colonies. He was not so much concerned with making Iceland purely independent, if association with another country would help her; but he insisted that all internal affairs should be under her own control, and that she should also have a voice in matters of international policy where she was concerned. The Althing, he maintained, should have the same rights in the affairs of Iceland, as the Danish Parliament had in the affairs of Denmark; that a complete separation of the finances of the two nations should be made by Royal decree; that no resolutions affecting the administration of Iceland should be made law until considered and passed by the Althing.

Among the many reforms in home affairs that he sought, was an efficient nation-wide system of education, which had been seriously neglected. The old grammar school needed reorganising and the whole system elevating to a higher level. As an example of his forward policy he advocated the establishment of a medical, a law, and a theological school, thus making the Government responsible and giving them power over three very essential national services. In suggesting a medical school he was decades ahead of the politicians of other countries, for his proposals included a staff of State-paid physicians. This policy was not carried out in his life-time, but is to some extent incorporated in present-day practice.

By 1873 Jón Sigurdsson's influence had become so strong that a progressive policy was everywhere growing up. Perhaps the most important step till then, one showing how powerful the national spirit had become, was the great meeting held at Thingvellir by the Thodvinafelag, *i.e.*, the Society of Friends of the People, of which Sigurdsson was President. It was there proposed to ask the King of Denmark to grant a constitution to Iceland on the thousandth anniversary of the colonisation of the country, which would take place the following year. The King granted the constitution on 5th January, 1874. By this the Althing was granted legislative powers together with the King, in matters concerning Iceland, and a special minister for Iceland was appointed, to be resident in Copenhagen.

We are told that "for all the benefits which this conferred, the country was chiefly indebted to Jón Sigurdsson." The Althing had now obtained legislative power and control of finances.

When the new Althing commenced its work, Icelanders were unacquainted with parliamentary procedure. It was Jón Sigurdsson who put matters in order and gave to the Althing the character and form it has since retained.

The amount of labour that he got through gives an excellent idea, not only of his extraordinary mental vigour, but also of his physical strength. His literary production was astonishingly great. No aspect of this phase that could contribute to his country's welfare was overlooked. In every case he brought to bear upon the task a masterly and comprehensive understanding. One of the most extensive and important of his literary labours is the Icelandic Collection of Laws in seventeen volumes. In this work documents are not merely reproduced but generally accompanied by instructive notes of great importance to the legal history of Iceland. No one, it is said, will undertake to write of that period without consulting this work. With indefatigable energy and at considerable personal expense, he collected all the manuscripts, documents, letters and records relating to the affairs of Iceland.

There can be no doubt that his literary services to Iceland were as important as his services as a statesman. No other person possessed so great a knowledge of the history of the island from the beginning until the date of Jón Sigurdsson's death.

Nor had he any reason to complain of the gratitude of his countrymen. From the beginning of his public career his sincerity and ability were recognised and applauded. No other Icelander had, for instance, so many verses sung in his praise during his lifetime. Icelandic poets at home and abroad vied with each other in acknowledging his worth.

He was President of the Althing in nearly every session from 1841 to 1879, and it became customary to refer to him as "the President" as an indication that he was the first and Chief of Icelanders.

His frankness allowed him never to violate what he regarded as his nation's good; and so little did he care for popularity when principle was at stake, that more than once he sided with the Danish Government against the wishes of his followers. It is surprising, however, that towards his old age he had to sell his magnificent library to pay his debts. These debts were not contracted through extravagance, unless spending his money for the benefit of his country can be regarded in that light, for he was an excellent economist.

It is regrettable to know that this splendid man died after much suffering. His demise took place in Denmark and his remains were carried to Iceland and buried in Reykjavík churchyard. His tomb is marked by a simple monument inscribed with the words "Iceland's favourite son. Her honour and Her shield."

Professor Willard Fiske, who knew Jón well, said, after his death, that through him "the national rights of Iceland are secured for all time to come, and the steady progress of his country, as the ages roll on, will form the most fitting monument to Jón Sigurdsson."

The demonstration that I witnessed in Reykjavík shows that Iceland in its present period of prosperity still feels keenly her debt to her greatest son, and takes delight in acknowledging it. The long procession formed to commemorate his life and death eventually left the Square where the wreath had been laid before the statue of this splendid patriot, and marched silently to the cemetery to lay two more wreaths upon his grave.

If his shade witnessed this ceremony it must have felt very satisfied with all the effort he had put forth during his arduous life; Iceland was now among the most prosperous nations in the world; rich, not only in material wealth, but also in youth, ambition and ability; and, above all, quite independent, with its own President and Prime Minister.

Briton and the United States of America recognise the change in the political status of Iceland, and have established consular envoys in Reykjavík, the British representative being a minister. Sweden, Norway and Russia have also sent political representatives where previously they had only consuls.

Thus has been fulfilled all and more than Jón Sigurdsson fought for; and in addition to seeing his nation freed from all foreign restraint, his shade may have the pleasant realisation, that the relations, political and commercial, between Icelanders and Danes have for a long time been excellent.

CHAPTER 6

CONSTITUTION

I was in Reykjavík at the General Election on 30th June, 1946, and was able to observe how these people behave during a big national crisis. Having witnessed general elections in several other countries, I was in the position of making useful comparisons. Icelanders came through very well, although they are keen politicians.

For several weeks preceding Election Day the air had been literally filled with the sound of various loud-speakers in different parts of the city, especially in Austurvöllur, the square in which stands the House of Parliament. Halls were packed night after night by attentive audiences listening to the candidates as they outlined their policies and made their promises. In no instance did I see any excitement, nothing but good order prevailing. It was obvious that no matter how enthusiastic Icelanders may be, they have considerable self-control.

Their tranquility, however, disguises their strong feelings, and it is doubtful if any country in the world has stronger political sentiments. Among such a well-read people, everybody is more or less acquainted with the different views of the political parties, especially as Communism has grown sufficiently powerful to claim seats in the Cabinet.

This year feeling ran more than averagely high because only two years had elapsed since Iceland had obtained complete independence, and for the first time in centuries controlled her own foreign policy. This independence does not sit lightly on their shoulders and it has yet to be proved that they can bear so expensive a burden. For 130,000 people to maintain Consulates in the capitals of several big countries, must be a severe strain on their financial resources. It is like a municipal borough in

England having to finance this expensive enterprise, for enterprise it really is.

A large number of important citizens are not quite sure whether after all it might not prove better if Iceland once more became dependent in foreign affairs on a more powerful country, such as Britain or the United States of America, the latter being much favoured. The suggestion is that Iceland become a sort of forty-ninth State. On the other hand the Communists favour Russia, from whom they derive, not only their inspiration, but also, it is believed, their policy.

The constitutional history of Iceland has been very varied. When the settlement originally began each chieftain was ruler of his own territory and adopted, usually, the system he had used before he came to Iceland. In the year 930 the people agreed to enforce the same laws for the whole country. This proved an almost insuperable difficulty for some time, as chieftains were not always ready to yield to the dictates of the lawmakers when the judgment was not according to their wishes. However, in course of time the Althing proved too strong for law-breakers, and the first Icelandic Commonwealth was founded and lasted, with slight change, for more than three hundred years.

There were certain defects in the old Republic which do not exist in the new one. In those days chieftainship was inherited and could be bought and sold. Today every member of the community has equal rights and, man or woman, may attain the highest position in the land by their own merits. Iceland was one of the first countries to give equal rights to women.

The temporary constitution at present prevailing (a new and permanent one is being formed) prohibits the introduction of any laws giving special rights connected with nobility, title and rank. Titles and nobility do not exist.

So democratic is the constitution that it outdoes even that of the United States of America. Whereas, the American Constitution gives its President absolute power of veto, in Iceland the power is vested in the Minister, the President having no responsibility in Governments affairs.

He is chosen by the nation through direct election for a period of four years, and is, of course, the head of the nation and "the first gentleman" in the land; but he is completely bound to parliament in the formation of Government and the choice of Ministers.

The tightness of the present constitutional system has eliminated the old weaknesses which laid it open to interference from outside, eventually making it subject to Norwegian and later to Danish rule. Of course, Iceland can never hope to defend itself against a powerful aggressor; but in a sense this weakness, combined with its important geographical location, is the country's strength, as other nations will, in their own interests, arise in its defence if necessary.

There is good reason for believing that Iceland will strive always to retain independence, because of the severe lessons she has been taught by the two countries to whom she has been subordinated—Norway and Denmark. Norway, after possessing her, succeeded gradually in so altering Icelandic laws that eventually the judicial and legislative power passed entirely into the hands of the King. Later, Denmark applied these powers with terrible ruthlessness, and the memory will never be effaced in Iceland. Nor has such fear been allayed by the British and American Occupation of 1940. Iceland's logical position during the war was that of strict neutrality, for invasion by any of the belligerents, no matter how well-intentioned, naturally laid it open to bombing by the enemy. As a matter of fact the Nazis did bomb the east coast, but did little damage.

Icelanders were not to know exactly what would happen to their chief city when the British built their airfield on its outskirts, and must have viewed the prospects with dread. "Pin pointing" has never been so perfect that one knew exactly where a bomb would fall, and it still looks pretty obvious that had the Germans attempted to bomb the British airfield at Reykjavík, the town would not have escaped serious damage. As it is events turned out very well and the British redeemed their promise to hand over the airfield to the Icelanders complete with equipment and experts to help them work it until they could do the job themselves. I was in Reykjavík on Saturday, 6th July, 1946, on that occasion. It took five years to complete the airfield and it passed into the hands of Iceland, complete with direction tower, fire-stations, runways, accommodation for over 100 guests, wireless apparatus and other installations. The entire undertaking places Iceland definitely on the map so far as commercial aviation is concerned, with an equipment far exceeding any possibility of her own to have installed unaided. Thus again did Iceland benefit by the war.

Britain promised to present the airport to the Icelandic Government immediately the war ended. The promise was repeated by Notes from the British Government, October 1944, and was carried out without delay. The Icelandic Prime Minister, Ólafur Thors, to whom the British Minister, Sir Gerald Shepherd, handed the specially made silver key as a token of possession, referred to this fact, and expressed the gratitude and appreciation of his countrymen for this splendid action on the part of one of the greatest nations in the world to the smallest.

Not only was the airport presented, but to ensure that the recipients would derive the greatest immediate benefit from it, a staff of airmen was left with it to instruct the Icelanders how to use it. The wish was expressed that the Icelanders might find it as great a help to them in peace as it had proved to the Allies in the war, especially the war in the Atlantic. No attempt was made by the British to make the Icelanders feel that they were receiving charity, it being fully recognised that the part they played in helping to win the war entitled them to such consideration. They had, one way and another, earned the airfield, and that is the way they themselves look at it. Later on, March, 1947, they received a similar gift from the American

Government, although that airport has no concrete runways like the British one.

The importance of Iceland as an aerial centre is summed up in the German reference to Iceland as "the unsinkable Aircraft Carrier." In the Spring of 1939 Nazi Germany sent a commission to the island to negotiate for air bases, but received a curt refusal. The Nazi story was that they required airfields for civilian and commercial purposes; but the Icelanders were unwilling to run the risk, and in diplomatic terms, sent Hitler about his business.

This was a bold step on the part of a helpless country, and showed a degree of courage lacking in a number of larger countries who trembled and negotiated with the German bully. This refusal certainly proved of untold value to the Allies. Had Iceland acceded to the later request of Germany, that it be given an opportunity to offer tenders for public works, with a promise of cheaper offers than anybody else, Iceland would have been invaded by a bevy of Nazi technical experts whose aim would have been to secure the country for Hitler. The Icelandic Cabinet were not to be caught napping, and overtures were again rejected. The result was that the position of the Germans in the Atlantic became precarious and finally impossible; and the war was doubtless greatly shortened in duration.

The ceremony of handing over the airport was very impressive and attended by a large concourse of Icelanders, including the President. At the conclusion of the ceremony the British Commanding Officer made a symbolic flight from the aerodrome as a further token that it now was the sole property of Iceland. The wish expressed by the British Minister that this gift might still further cement the friendship of the two countries is sure to be fulfilled, and Britain comes out of the deal with flying colours. Any ill-feeling that may have remained in the breasts of Icelandic isolationists must have been entirely dissipated by this generous gesture and magnificent gift.

Long before 1939 Iceland was an object of interest

on the part of Britain and America as well as of Germany the Germans taking great pains to win the people over to their point of view. There is plenty of evidence that Hitler took steps to prepare the way should it be necessary to land German troops in Iceland, although this was not encouraged by the Icelandic Government, and probably not realised by the ordinary citizen. The fact remains, however, that for several years previous to the outbreak of hostilities German and Austrian "Tourists" were to be met with all over Iceland.

Even such isolated parts as Vatnajökull, the great glacier, did not escape their attention, at least one important German expedition devoting considerable time to exploring it and we may be sure, its surroundings and strategical advantages. There is every reason for believing that Britain was not unaware of Hitler's intentions and took steps to counteract them.

There is still a belief that Icelanders were pro-Nazi; but this is true only of some of them, and that can be said of other countries. The chief fear of Icelandic democrats has been of Communism, and that fear is as real today as it was before the war. Rightly or wrongly, every anti-ally and anti-social action is attributed to Communists. One never hears the word Nazi.

The position of both British and American servicemen was certainly unsettled while I was there. No one seemed to notice them, and this alone must have made them feel uncomfortable. One would suppose that, since the Armies of Occupation had so advantageously changed the economic life of Icelanders, they would have been welcome. According to the servicemen themselves they were quite unwanted. I speak only of those whom I met in Reykjavík, as one seldom saw them elsewhere.

There was undoubtedly some sort of feeling against servicemen in Reykjavík, although the natives strenuously denied it. It was impossible to believe that both British and American airmen and sailors had conspired to misrepresent the situation. None of them cared to walk alone at night, and it was a habit, encouraged by the military authorities, to wear mufti when off duty. Late in August I met a number of young British sailors returning from the fair-grounds; all were dressed in civilian clothes. They assured me that there was serious danger of their being attacked if they wore uniform. These mysterious assaults always occurred on dark nights and in isolated places. The culprits seem never to have been caught, which was surely as mysterious as the attacks, victims being struck on the head with some heavy instrument. Sometimes more serious methods were adopted.

While strolling down the main thoroughfare of Reykjavík one afternoon, I saw a young American officer with whom I had conversed in Hotel Borg. Approaching him from behind—he was looking in a shop window—I spoke to him, and he swung round nervously and was obviously startled. I asked what he was afraid of.

"You," he replied with a sigh of relief.

"Why me?" I enquired with surprise.

"Oh," he continued, "I don't like this darned place; one never feels safe in it. It gets on my nerves."

He went on to explain that only the previous night mysterious shots had been fired at some American jeeps just outside Reykjavík. "If this sort of thing goes on," he said fiercely, "our Commanding Officer threatens to come down and clean up the town."

After convincing myself that the young man believed he spoke the truth, I mentioned the conversation to some informed Icelanders, but they declared they knew nothing about the matter, and if it happened it was certainly kept from the Press. They were all of the opinion that the responsible parties may have been Communists, desirous of disturbing relationships between the Icelandic Government and the Allies, but all these critics were definitely anti-communist. It was further pointed out by my Icelandic friends that these attacks might have been caused by British and American servicemen, who were certainly not always on the best of terms with each other. The shooting at the jeeps was not easy to account for in terms of Icelanders, because they are practically without arms, which can be procured only by Government consent; but against this is the well-known fact that gunmen simply laugh at such restrictions. Similar incidents were just as inconclusive. These affairs were more difficult to understand as Icelanders readily admitted that the Occupation had enriched the country beyond their wildest dreams, and raised it in a few years from a relatively poor condition to an extremely rich one.

On the whole they grew to like the invaders and many sincere friendships, and not a few marriages, were contracted. There was, of course, some illegitimacy, and it fell to the lot of some of the Lutheran clergy to settle disputes that arose from these affairs. One of these gentlemen assured me that there was a decided difference in the attitude of the putative fathers. Americans, he said, much more readily admitted parentage than Britishers, who were always suspicious and more prepared to dispute the case. I suggested that the better financial circumstances of the Americans was the cause, but he attributed it to some inherent psychological characteristic.

Both world wars had a beneficial effect in Iceland, especially the recent one. The First World War considerably weakened relationships between Iceland and Denmark. 1918 was one of the most momentous years in the history of Iceland. On 30th November of that year, a law was adopted by both Iceland and Denmark creating the kingdom of Iceland, with equal rights with Denmark. Although little notice was taken of this event by the outside world, owing to the more pressing matters arising from the Peace, it marked the real liberation and independence of Iceland.

That war also greatly altered Iceland's economic relations which had hitherto been more stable but less progressive. Cut off from Britain through Germany's naval activities, the island was compelled to develop her own communications with the outside world, especially the United States.

This led to a surprising expansion of Iceland's sea communications and she was forced to make an efficient mercantile marine. The famous Icelandic Steamship Company was established and, although not a Government undertaking, it is national in the sense that one-third of the population subscribed to its formation. Icelanders are natural sailors and the line was a great success.

This extension of trade relations considerably affected Britain, which had hitherto been closely associated with Iceland in a business way. It let in other countries, notably the United States, which, as far as I could judge, is still highly favoured; but this cannot be attributed to anti-British feeling. If favouritism is shown to America it is because of a number of national characteristics which favour the Americans.

For instance, their servicemen were better paid, better clothed, better housed and more considerately treated than the British, and on the whole they were better educated. When the British forces arrived they did a good deal of non-military work, while America employed local labour. As one Icelander put it: "Americans were real soldiers and the British were not." Furthermore, the Icelanders preferred the more genial relationships that prevailed between American officers and the rankers. They were less snobbish than British officers, and not less efficient. Their more restrained and disciplined attitude made the Icelander feel that the British rank and file were not so friendly as the American rank and file and they reacted accordingly.

Icelanders definitely dislike class distinction. A people so intimately related to each other naturally would.

One thing is clear: in many respects Americans are still preferred to British. Icelanders like their progressive and forceful business methods, and find their goods reliable. If ever Britain displaces them it will be because of lower transport costs giving British goods a financial advantage.

My personal experience of British goods in Iceland was distressing. The day after my arrival at Reykjavík I bought a new hat because my own had been ruined by the sea.

I naturally bought a British made hat and paid for it an exchange equivalent to 51s. 6d. In less than two months the hat was disgraceful although I had occasion to wear it seldom. On returning to Britain I communicated with the Board of Trade as I had been unable to extract, even from the agent of the hat manufacturer, the address of the firm. My intention was merely to draw their attention to the defects of the hat, concluding that they would give a satisfactory explanation, replace the hat with a more worthy article, and see that in future Iceland received a better-class article.

The firm in question passed the hat and my complaint to a higher authority who concluded that the fault must have been due to the brilliantine I had been using. Incidentally I use none but British manufactured brilliantine and a good standard make, plenty of which seemed procurable in Reykjavík.

The upshot of all my trouble was to receive a communication from the Central Price Regulation Committee stating that while the Board of Trade thanked me for the trouble I had taken in bringing this matter to their notice, they were convinced that the firm was not to blame but only the manufacturers of the brilliantine. They were satisfied that the hatters could continue to hold their own in the face of acute foreign competition.

I am not convinced, however, as I was assured by a firm of hatters in Edinburgh that one of the best British firms of hatters had had a consignment thrown on their hands by Icelanders, who preferred American hats. I am, alas, still without my hat, as the firm that manufactured it and to which I sent it as proof of the reliability of my complaint, never returned it to me. It was all too obvious that American hats are extremely popular in Iceland, and it looks as if they will continue to be so.

Americans are given preference over Britishers in more ways than one. I talked with several young Icelanders in various parts of the country who had been educated abroad, most of them in American universities, a few in Copenhagen none in Britain. I met only one Icelander who considered sending his son to Britain for his higher education. He was a highly placed executive in the Icelandic shipping world, and he lived several years in Leith, Scotland, and was therefore familiar with British ways. His intention was to send his son to Oxford, but was at the time unable to obtain permission and was thinking of sending the youth to a good English provincial university until a favourable opportunity made it possible for him to enter Oxford.

Icelanders are keen on technical education, largely owing to the rapid development of their water power. There are several large engineering undertakings in process, but in none of them is a Britisher employed, the engineers being without exception, either American, Danish or Icelandic. But the Olfusá bridge, quite the finest in the country, was constructed by British engineers.

Four political parties contested the 1946 election. A few years ago there were only two. 1930 saw the birth of the Communist party, which grew rapidly after 1935, and was, for a time, the opposition. Later on, the Progressive or Farmers Party, at one time the most powerful party, became the opposition, and still is. The other parties are the Conservative and the Socialist, the latter being comparable with the British Labour Party, and the former with the old British Radicals, with a strong flavour of socialism. The most conservative party is the Progressive.

It would be difficult for a Britisher to evaluate the true political nature of the Icelandic Conservative Party. I had a good deal to do with many of its leading supporters and found them much nearer socialism than many British Labour leaders. They stand for free trade and capitalism, but support the socialisation of essential public services.

The Press is a truly powerful organ in Iceland, and distinctly partisan, the moderate and Conservative newspapers attracting the largest number of readers. The newspapers are very well got up and speak with great freedom; but on the whole Icelanders are fairly tolerant of other people's opinions, although inclined, it is said, to bigotry in politics, believing 100 per cent. in free speech. I attended some of the political meetings and, although I did not understand a word of what was said, was impressed by the earnestness and eloquence of the speakers. The Icelandic tongue is sonorous, musical, soft and smooth to the ear, and appears capable of expressing every shade of thought. This fact must account to some extent for its survival with so much of its original purity. None of the speakers showed great emotion, the appeal being to the reason.

It struck me, a member of a country with a population of nearly fifty millions, as remarkable that this little nation should deal with its internal organisation with all the enthusiasm and dignity of a first-class nation, and with a distinct international flavour! It speaks volumes for their efficiency that they should have not merely mayors and town councillors, but also a Government with six Ministers of State, *i.e.*, a Prime Minister; a Minister of Foreign Affairs; a Minister of Trade and Labour; a Minister of Justice; a Minister of Finance; a Minister of Education; and a Minister of Communications.

Constitutional power is divided into three: legislative, executive and judiciary. In the main, three bodies exercise the following powers: Parliament the legislative, the President in conjunction with the Ministers the executive, and the Judges the judiciary.

There are fifty-two members of Parliament, elected in three ways—by direct election, proportional election, and by what is called compensatory or equalising election. "Compensatory election" exists because the electoral system does not permit suitable proportional representation, eleven members being co-opted in relevant proportions among the four parties. Citizens of both sexes are eligible as voters at the age of twenty-one. Change of address does not, as in Britain, disqualify the elector for one moment. When I informed them that because I had removed from London to Edinburgh and had not been in Edinburgh long enough to be placed on the Voters' List, that if I had wished to vote I should have had to do so in London, a distance of four hundred miles away, they were amazed at the stupidity and injustice of it.

All of the political parties are very active and strive strenuously for power. At one time the Farmers Party predominated and almost entirely dictated the national policy, notwithstanding that only one-third of the nation are devoted to that industry. More and more the wealth of the country has depended upon the fisheries, and fishermen constitute only about 15 per cent. of the population, but they live for the most part in the towns.

Gradually political influence has swung from the country districts to the towns, in which reside nearly 60 per cent. of the population. Iceland is therefore not a country of farmers as so many people think. In Reykjavík, where lives at least one-third of the nation, the Progressives number only about 1,000 votes.

The 1946 election shows that the Progressive vote is still declining, while Labour and Conservative vote is increasing, with Communism stationary. The constitution of the present Ministry must seem almost grotesque, containing two Conservatives, two Socialists and two Communists, notwithstanding that the Socialists and Conservatives are definitely opposed to Communism. No other country outside of Soviet Russia has felt the force of Communism more profoundly. It is by no means ideological only, as it has proven on several occasions. Some time ago the Conservatives wanted to reduce wages to avoid inflation, but the Communists objected and threatened to call a strike. Realising their power and desirous of avoiding the calamity this action would have brought to pass, the Government adopted its present policy of improving equipment.

Iceland is one of the most powerful co-operative countries in the world, and co-operative societies are to be found in even the smallest town. They are particularly strong among farmers, who really started the system. Their political strength exists largely in their firm co-operation.

The duration of Parliament, according to the present

Constitution, is four years; but the Government has the power to shorten it and if necessary to dissolve it.

The responsibilities of the Government are considerable, owing to the large extension of nationalisation and there is every indication that fresh obligations will be added. At present the Government holds a monopoly on various products and imports, including tobacco, matches, wines, potatoes and lemons. In addition there are, under its control, such large public undertakings as telephones, post office, roads, various social services, including institutions of a therapeutic and charitable kind.

The Government has also determined to modernise farming, which is almost invariably conservative and therefore non-progressive. No farming community is more firmly wedded to tradition than these people, and the consequences are none too good. The younger generation dislike the occupation, and the Government realises that unless they can offer them greater inducements they will migrate to the towns more and more. This would undoubtedly prove disastrous. One strange feature is that the farmers themselves know they are behind the times, and by no means obtaining the best results; but it is obvious that they will have to be compelled to change their methods. As far as I could judge, and I went all round the island, with the exception of the north-west, where I understand farming is much the same as elsewhere, and saw little more than potato growing and hay-making. Hay-making seems to be a passion with the farmers, who doubtless must do it to feed their cattle during the winter months. But the fact remains that from the day of my arrival in the beginning of June, until my departure towards the middle of September, hay-making was going on unremittingly everywhere.

The British Consul at Akureyri assured me that he was growing excellent strawberries and several species of British flowers in his garden, and that with little effort a great deal of improvement could be made in Icelandic agriculture. But this is also, I found, the opinion of others from abroad.

By buying agricultural implements and selling them to farmers, the Government has done much already to bring back to the farms the young men and women who had refused to work the old hand methods. It was too exhausting and uncongenial, and lacked the appeal that machinery has in this machine age. The Government takes great care that no middle man steps in to add to the cost of these implements, no private individual being allowed to act as agent.

The Government is also trying to find minerals and anyone who opens a mine must hand it over to the Government. It is well known that there is both iron and gold in the mountains, but not in sufficient quantities to make them workable without the introduction of the most modern methods. To encourage mining the Government is prepared to give licences to anyone willing to work them on this principle. Icelandic spar, which is already a paying proposition, is sometimes worked by the Government, and sometimes by private companies under licence.

Lack of coal has always been a serious matter in Iceland, although there are mines on the north coast which were worked a great deal during the war when no supplies were coming from Britain. That these may never be a paying proposition is, today, no serious matter because of the increasing harnessing of water power and the use of hot water from the natural springs.

Soon after my arrival in Iceland I visited the House of Parliament and even sat in the President's chair in the Senate Room. The entire setting of this historic building, inside as well as out, may be described as severe. There is none of the ostentation which usually characterises these buildings, of which Britain is perhaps, the most striking example. The florid "gilded chamber" of the House of Lords finds in Iceland its antithesis; and just as the one chamber arose out of class distinction of a most egregious kind, the other speaks firmly of a people who have always been simple and unassuming. The fourteen members of the Senate, or Upper Chamber, have the gratification of knowing that they hold their places because they have won the confidence of their fellow citizens, and not by unjustified favour.

There is a reflection of all this in the circumstances which arose when Iceland sought a basis for its Constitution. They found nothing in Britain to help them, for the simple reason that it has no written Constitution. Iceland had, therefore, to turn elsewhere and found, partly in the Declaration of Independence of the United States of America, and partly in the teachings of the French lawyer Montesquieu and the French Declaration of the Revolution, *des droit de l'homme et du citoyen*, what they wanted.

Iceland is taking up aviation with great zest, planes connecting it with the outside world leaving the airfield at Reykjavík daily.

CHAPTER 7

MAKING FISHING SMACKS

WHEN the smallness of the population of Iceland is considered, there is naturally a tendency to regard it more as a municipality than as a State, and any undertakings it may embark upon are in danger of being looked upon as examples of municipalisation and not of nationalisation. It is necessary to be free from this notion, otherwise Iceland, from a Governmental point of view will be gravely misunderstood.

No municipality in Britain has to control an area as large as Iceland, and, of course, no international affairs fall within its jurisdiction. Even to compare Iceland with the London County Council, with its tremendous population and vast financial responsibilities, would be a mistake. The difference of populations is admittedly staggering, but London is, after all, a very restricted area compared with Iceland, and again the international question does not arise. What I mean to say is that Iceland does not municipalise only, it nationalises, and some very important undertakings have been entered upon, especially during the last few years. This tendency to nationalisation has doubtless been stimulated by the growth of Socialism and Communism, and as those political parties continue to keep strong, it will be accentuated.

National Banks have existed for some time, and three main Banks belong to the Government; the Savings Banks, which belong to the corporate bodies such as various Benefit Societies and Trades Unions, remaining free. But since they are all co-operative in nature, they are not far removed from nationalisation. The tendency is to bring all banking into alignment and in time all Banks will be directly under State control. The post-office, including telegrams, telephones and radio, is strictly a national enterprise.

GULFOSS

Famous waterfall

Icelandic scenery. The author standing on the edge of a boiling pool 1946

6.

GODAFOS

DELTIFOSS

1946

Showing the author

During the last two years the Government has struck out along a new and unusual line, one of tremendous possibilities for a maritime nation: it has begun to build ships, and has already made such headway that it has decided to become a "middle man" purchasing ships from other countries including Britain, and Sweden, and selling them.

I was invited by the manager to visit the ship-building yard just outside Reykjavík, and the repair works, just inside the precincts of the city, to see how these matters are being handled. I daresay that anyone connected with shipbuilding on the Clyde or Newcastle-on-Tyne would have been amused at the smallness of what, to Icelanders, is evidently regarded as a considerable undertaking. Four fishing trawlers were being built, one of which was nearly completed; the entire shipyard, therefore, being no bigger than one that might be laid down in Britain by a very small company.

But the job was being done efficiently and there is no doubt, judging from the comments of experts, that in building 60 or 70-ton trawlers Icelanders have very little to learn. The average price of these vessels is about £10,000, so that the profits cannot be large—as yet; but Iceland has given up the habit of looking at things from the standpoint of today only, and is attaching a lot of meaning to the future and to posterity. Iceland intends to live a long time, and means to grown up healthy. It is therefore leaving nothing to chance, and even if the beginnings are small, the final aspects may become very large and important.

These boats are wooden, the timber—sturdy oak—being brought from Canada and the United States. Parts of the hulls will be covered with metal, but the only part wholly so will be the deck house. Even to the uninitiated such as I, it was apparent that the workmen knew their jobs and did them with efficiency and zest, and the Manager was very satisfied.

I was somewhat surprised to find that in the workshops

F

the repair of motor cars was undertaken, showing that the State means to ramify its controls into very important fields. At present few industrial fields can, in Iceland, be more remunerative than that of the automobile, for every Icelander who can afford one will get it if at all possible. Some of the prices that they pay are fabulous when calculated in kronur, and when a proud owner tells you, with a grin, that he paid 50,000 kronur for a Dodge or a Chrysler, he will readily admit that he got it through the black-market and was lucky to do so. This means they have paid well over 100 per cent. more than the normal market value. To repair these numerous vehicles should bring much profit to the Treasury.

The Government has run two sea-going vessels very successfully for several years, but the trawlers it sells to private owners. It has been buying trawlers from other countries for the same purpose. At present it has no intention of nationalising the fishing industry, but the thin end of the wedge is apparent when it is remembered that the Government has intimated that if the trawlers are not bought by the people they will entirely nationalise their ship-building industry.

Britain is certainly losing nothing by this extensive development of Icelandic fishing. Recently orders were placed in England and Scotland for thirty 600-ton trawlers, at a cost of about £110,000 each. Half of them have been ordered by private firms and half by municipal authorities. The Reykjavík City Council has ordered five, the Nordfjördur and Akureyri Town Councils two each. Mr. Thórdur Ólafsson, one of Iceland's outstanding authorities on trawlers and fishing, informed me that the orders were placed in Britain because there they are assured of the finest workmanship.

CHAPTER 8

GEYSERS AND WATERFALLS

SEVENTY-FOUR miles north-east of Reykjavík lies Great Geysir, the famous so-called "monarch" of hot springs. To be able to form a correct judgment on such unusual phenomena as geysers and fumeroles, it is necessary to see more than one. "Great Geysir" was the first of these remarkable hot water spouts to be discovered by Europeans, although they must have been known to the Redman, the Maori, and the inhabitants of Madagascar and two or three eastern lands, long before the white man gazed upon this masterpiece of Iceland.

It is twenty-three years since I visited the thermal region of New Zealand, and seventeen since I was at Yellowstone Park, Wyoming; but I have no hesitation in saying that the thermal phenomena of both these countries were more impressive than those of Iceland. Iceland, New Zealand, and America are the order in which as a rule, these remarkable areas are regarded: Iceland because she is the oldest in order of discovery; New Zealand because her's is the most extraordinary, partly because of compactness and partly because of its indescribable charm and beauty; and America because Yellowstone Park undoubtedly presents, in its immense area, the largest, most powerful, and most numerous of these strange manifestations of nature.

When I visited the thermal area around Lake Rotomahana, New Zealand, the Waimungu Geyser had ceased to function, and in its place there was a large pool of boiling water; but it has since renewed its activities. From it ran a hot stream which later on converged with a cold one, and a person could actually stand between them and place one hand in cold water and the other in hot at the same time!

Owing to the volcanic origin of geysers they are unreliable, and one can never be sure when they will cease to operate, or recur after a period of quiescence. This has been the case with Great Geysir. It has varied tremendously in power and frequency, sometimes ceasing for several years. In 1809 it seems to have been in the habit of shooting a column of water and steam at least 100 feet every thirty hours. In 1815 its power increased, and it shot every six hours and its columns attained 150 feet. Its highest shot, recorded with a quadrant over all time, was 212 feet.

Then for some reason it ceased to operate for several years, and when Olive Murray Chapman visited it in 1929 she neither saw nor expected it to work. On the other hand, when W. Bisiker, F.R.G.S., saw it exactly thirty years before, it obliged him with no less than six fine shots in fourteen hours. In 1881, John Coles, F.R.A.S., F.R.G.S., was disappointed at the poor showing it made, although he waited patiently for something more. He would have found little to have justified the trouble of his journey to this remote spot had not Strokkur, a much less famous geyser today spouted to a height of 100 feet. Strokkur is a close neighbour of Geysir, and has suffered more than once by his whimsicalities. Thus, in 1896, an earthquake made Great Geysir so active that it rendered Strokkur impotent, and it has never since regained its lost reputation. Strokkur is rather plebeian in its tastes as it will often oblige if fed with turf, but Great Geysir demands nothing less than soap, and plenty of it.

It was because of soap that I visited Great Geysir. The news having spread abroad that he was to have his desired feast, a large party of people forgathered from all parts to see the result. A considerable quantity of soap had to be dropped into his vent, and after about four hours Geysir responded in a kind of spasmodic way. The day was dull and wet and there was little to encourage either him or his admirers, but he certainly seemed anxious to do his best for them. For about three-quarters of an hour he made desperate efforts to reach high, and it is probable that he did attain 90 feet once or twice; but what he lacked in height he made up for in quantity, as during that period he made numerous shots.

A geyser is a natural spring or fountain which discharges into the air a column of heated water or steam. The Icelandic word "geysir" means gusher or rager. Great Geysir is situated in a broad, barren valley, at the foot of a range of hills from 300 to 400 feet in height, and this setting adds a necessary feature to the scene. One feels that geysers, which throw a good deal of siliceous sinter, a by no means attractive-looking chemical, should have a severe setting, and Great Geysir has. In its calm periods Great Geysir appears as a circular pool about sixty feet in diameter and four feet in depth, the colour of the water being sea-green, and always too hot for anyone to put his hand in without being burned. It is usually about 188°F. In the centre of the basin is the vent hole, and raised around it in all directions lies its silica mantle.

He does not lack suitable company, as it is computed that within a radius of two miles there are upwards of one hundred hot springs, varying vastly in character and dimensions. These peculiarities give personality to these monsters, and they are regarded with affection and pride by Icelanders. These emotions can never be lost, even when the former glory of the weird phenomena has departed. Strokkur is a case in point. Twice since the earthquake of 1896 he has done a fine job, and may any day decide to return to regular employment. It is to his credit that one of these two eruptions came as the result of soap; and there is a possibility that he will become as aristocratic as Great Geysir seems always to have been.

The Rev. Baring Gould saw Great Geysir operate after one of the quiet spells, and judging from his colourful account of the event, Geysir must have behaved much more impressively than when I saw him. Baring Gould's graphic account is worth recounting. "Presently," he writes, "a dome of water rose in the basin and fell again, immediately to be followed by a fresh bell, which sprang into the air full 40 feet high, accompanied by a roaring burst of steam. Instantly the fountain began to play with the utmost violence, a column rushed up to the height of 90 to 100 feet into the sky with mighty volumes of white steam-clouds rolling about it, and swept off by the breeze to fall in torrents of hot rain. Jets and lines of water tore their way through the cloud, or leaped high above its domed mass. The earth trembled and throbbed during the explosion; then the column sank and started up again, dropped once more, and seemed to be sucked back into the earth.

"We ran to the basin which was left dry, and looked down the bore at the water, which was bubbling at the depth of 16 feet. The diameter of the tube was found to be nine feet six inches. A plummet sank seventy-six feet."

It is gratifying to know Baring Gould was so fortunate. During my visit the explosions and thunderings were less noticeable. The reverend gentleman had probably never seen a geyser before and must have been filled with wonder. Geysir's action was merely a fair reward for the inconveniences Baring Gould must have experienced travelling to the scene. In his day there were no motor-cars to speed one over the rough hilly roads of loose stones, running perilously through mountainous country, often inexpressibly alluring in its crudeness, except where here and there an isolated farmhouse, surrounded by bright green fields, breaks the severity of the scene.

Among the many notabilities who have visited Great Geysir is William Jackson Hooker, F.L.S., who did so in the summer of 1809, calling at Thingvellir on the way. He gives a very comprehensive account of his experience and shows that at that time Strokkur could be more impressive than Great Geysir. It took the famous scientist six days to do the journey from Reykjavík, remaining only one day at Thingvellir en route. This is an excellent commentary on the difficulties of travel in Iceland in those days. Geysir is only seventy-four miles from Reykjavík; Herra Sigurjón Pjetursson, my host, motored me there in four hours. Thingvellir is not more than fifty miles from Great Geysir. It took Hooker three days to travel the thirty-one miles between the capital and Thingvellir, and two days from Thingvellir to Great Geysir.

Hooker was amply rewarded for the inconveniences of the journey, during which he slept in tents and was sometimes wet through with no opportunity to dry his clothes. The weather was excellent and Great Geysir was in a good mood, making several fine shots during the three days that he studied it. He calculates that its best effort reached 100 feet, and he was much delighted by the beauty of the scene, the sun shining brightly as Geysir vomited his vast columns of water.

The most interesting part of Hooker's narrative, however, is the remarkable demonstration by Strokkur, known at that time as the "new Geysir." Hooker had heard that this geyser often gave fine exhibitions, and in case it behaved favourably during his visit he placed his tent near enough not to miss it. On this occasion its showing outdid Great Geysir, who also behaved very well.

Strokkur acted without warning, and Hooker rushed to the door of his tent to see a sight which so overpowered him that it deprived him of the power to think of ascertaining its height and volume. But later he was able to make calculations, for during an hour and a half Strokkur threw uninterruptedly a column of water and steam to a height of not less than one hundred feet, with a body seventeen feet in diameter. The main difference between Strokkur and Great Geysir on this occasion was the tremendous force of the former. It appeared far to exceed the latter, and the column continued nearly to its summit as a compact body of water as regular in width and shape as when it first issued from the vent.

Hooker insists that he made no mistake in his calculations because a powerful breeze carried the immense column of steam that accompanied the eruption to one side, leaving the column of water in full view. Hooker threw into the vent great masses of siliceous rock, and was astonished to find that these were not only ejected, but shivered into fragments by the force of the uprising water. On applying a similar experiment to Great Geysir, the rocks were merely ejected.

Sir James Stanley appears to have been the first man to describe Strokkur and it was he who named it "new, Geysir."

It is not surprising that some "tall" stories should have originated about such remarkable phenomena as these thermal regions. Hooker mentions one which had been retailed by more than one visitor in the eighteenth century, and accepted even by Icelanders. It was to the effect that a species of bird was to be found in these hot springs, enjoying life as much as their more temperate brethren. These birds were said not only to float upon the surface of the hot water, but even to dive into it evidently with comfort and delight!

Imagination was so precise on this matter that we have on record a description of these prodigies, which were said to have the form and size of a duck and to be of a deep brown colour all over the body except for a conspicuous white ring round the eye. The bird is said sometimes to have remained so long under the water that it failed to reappear, which may account for the fact that none were there during Hooker's visit, nor do they seem to have appeared since! Hooker's statement that viewing the geysers gave him more pleasure than anything else during his visit to Iceland has been endorsed by more than one visitor. This, however, is a matter of opinion; but doubtless to a scientist interested, as Hooker was, in natural phenomena of an unusual kind, this amazing manifestation of natural force, at the time the only one of its kind known, must have appealed strongly to him.

For comparison let us consider the thermal regions of New Zealand and America.

In 1886 seven great geysers came into existence when mount Tarawera erupted. I have been on this mountain in the North Island of New Zealand and walked over the two Maori villages which lie buried beneath eighteen feet of lava. On this occasion water from these geysers, along with steam and mud were thrown eight hundred feet high for a period of four hours! There we have the world's record for geysers, brief though they lived.

In Yellowstone Park, Wyoming, U.S.A., there exist today various geysers on a large scale, some of which I have gazed upon. "Old Faithful," for instance, has won its name because of the regularity of its shots, which soar upward every sixty minutes to a height of 150 feet for five minutes. When I saw him he had delayed one minute beyond his usual time and made a special effort. Some say that he easily topped 150 feet on that occasion. But the "Beehive" reaches 220 feet with consistency. Indeed, several of these geysers (they number more than a hundred) render those of New Zealand and Iceland insignificant by comparison. Some of them have very distinct characteristics in the form and colour of their siliceous mounds, in the style of their eruptions and in the shape of their columns. "The Giantess" and "The Castle," both with definite personalities, as it were, reach 250 feet with ease.

But capping them all in size and magnificence of display is "Grand Geysir." If he alone existed Yellowstone Park would hold the record for this kind of phenomenon. When this geyser works, it seems as if some mighty artist fond of fireworks uses the only material at his disposal. Grand Geysir begins by filling his basin with boiling water, forming a well about twenty-five feet in diameter and having a visible depth of one hundred feet. The explosion is preceded by clouds of steam rushing up to a height of five hundred feet, the unbroken body of water that follows ascending in one gigantic column of ninety feet. From the apex of the column the monster radiates five jets, which shoot upwards until they are 250 feet from the ground! There is in geysers nothing to be compared with this, except it be one that I saw rushing upward from the centre of a small lake in a solid column about fifty feet high, seventy feet long and fourteen feet thick. It continued thus for several hours, and then took a well-earned rest before repeating the performance. The amount of water emitted by this geyser was immense, and it ran hot from the lake in a rapid stream.

The action of geysers is caused, it is believed (for science has never been quite sure of the cause) by a pressure of steam somewhere in the vent, which accumulates and forces the water above it out of the shaft.

One usually goes from Grand Geysir to Gullfoss, which lies, as the crow flies, about ten miles to the east. The journey is much longer by road, which has been made for convenience rather than for shortness of distance. Like so many of Iceland's roadways, it is full of differences, mostly on the awkward side. Icelanders deserve the greatest praise for what they have done with most difficult terrain. But there is charm, for these crude roads fit nicely into the general scenery. Occasionally one comes upon a smooth reddish brown section of the roadway, which affords comfortable travelling, and these are usually made of powdered lava.

Much of the way is less than what in England and France would be considered a cart track. But it cannot be helped and the modern car is so efficient that it can make light work of them.

The highway from Great Geysir to Gullfoss is among the worst in the country, and it is surprising the Government has not paid more attention to it. It is perhaps the most frequently-traversed highway by visitors to Iceland. One can only surmise that the authorities have some regard for the spirit of adventure which usually animates these tourists. They certainly get thrills and inconveniencies too; but they also get results.

Gullfoss, or "Golden Fall," has long been known as one of the most beautiful falls in Europe, and it ranks high in Iceland, a land of waterfalls, cataracts and cascades. It is part of the Southern Hvítá, an important river in south west Iceland. Hvítá means "White River," a name bestowed upon it because, flowing from a glacier, it is mixed with white clay. At the time of my visit this river was still the centre of sad interest. Some time before a terrible accident happened a few miles below the fall, through which three people lost their lives, including a women member of the Althing. I visited the scene of the accident through necessity, and it was obvious why the tragedy had occurred. It was a case of bad roads and bad planning. The track, for it could hardly be called anything else, leading from Geysir to Gullfoss, here took a sudden and dangerous turn on a steep declivity towards a bridge over the Hvítá, very awkwardly situated. All that was required to cause a motor car to pitch into the swiftly-flowing stream was a weak brake, mist, or a nervous driver. Once in the river nothing short of a miracle could save anyone shut in an automobile. The miracle did happen in this case, and two of the five passengers succeeded in getting out of the car and the stream.

Gullfoss is really a series of falls, or cataracts, rather than a single fall, and this greatly enhances its beauty. Its shape also adds to its attractiveness. Instead of making a single plunge in one direction, it consists of six or seven cascades before taking a definite turn to the main fall, where it plunges over the rim into a deep, narrow gorge about ninety feet below, and rushes madly away, hidden, for the main part, from view.

Because of its series of cascades Gullfoss cannot be compared with most other famous falls. I have often seen Niagara Falls, which dimensionally dwarfs Gullfoss, but it is impossible to compare them owing to their great difference. Niagara is divided into two mighty falls separated by a narrow strip of land. The American Fall is a straight drop of 167 feet, and has a width of well over 1,000 feet. The Canadian or "Horse Shoe Fall" has a drop of 158 feet and a width of 2,500 feet. The beautiful curve which gives rise to the term "Horse Shoe" is very symmetrical and this makes it by far the more interesting.

Something of the dimensional superiority of Niagara to Gullfoss can be formed when it is remembered that Gullfoss is only about 150 feet wide and drops about 130 feet in all. Yet Gullfoss is, in its way, as attractive as Niagara, for what the latter gains in size and weight the former gains in variety and beauty.

The gorges cannot, however, be compared. The vast mass of water that flows over the rims of Niagara creates one of the most awe-inspiring and thrilling gorges in the world. The waters rush impetuously for miles between rocky cliffs from two hundred to three hundred and fifty feet in height, until they reach the whirlpool, which, fitting into a kind of elbow in the gorge, twists and turns as the water endeavours to escape. There is also the additional advantage of being able to approach the foot of the falls in a steam launch until the spray becomes too dense and the course too dangerous to proceed. Gullfoss grants no such privilege.

But Nature has come to the rescue of the Icelandic falls, and when the sun shines the spray is lit with all the colours of the spectrum, forming lovely rainbows which change position every time the visitor moves. This alone transports one into a veritable fairy land, and makes one feel thankful to the gods for granting so unique an opportunity to see the lovely handiwork of nature.

I was more fortunate than some previous writers on Gullfoss, as a munber of them had the misfortune of visiting it in dull weather, depriving them of the rainbow effect.

I have seen all the principal waterfalls in Iceland: Dettifoss, Gufufoss, Múlafoss, Hjálparfoss, Öxaráfoss, Godafoss, Seljalandsfoss, as well as many smaller ones. Each has its individual appeal and all are examples of Iceland's wonderful natural resources, much of which is at present running to waste. The Government is fully alive to the value of this natural power and is harnessing it whenever possible.

Waterfalls are inevitable where there are mountains, and as Iceland is full of these collossi; there are myriads of waterfalls, especially when the snow is melting. On a journey from Budareyri to Egilstadir, on the east coast,

I was delighted by the many small falls and cateracts which ran gleefully down the mountain sides, adding enchantment to an already fascinating scene. But this is typical of a hundred valleys in this country. These small falls and cateracts add greatly to the impressiveness of the larger falls which every now and then burst upon the sight.

By many people Dettifoss is regarded as even more impressive than Gullfoss, but it is difficult to make a comparison. Dettifoss is a straight drop into the gorge below, and the gorge is much more imposing than that at Gullfoss. In all probability its volume of water is greater too, although it is not so wide; but being fed from Vatnajökull, in all likelihood the largest glacier in Europe, it is only to be expected that in quantity it would be supreme.

It was my good fortune to see Dettifoss on a perfect summer day, the sun shining brightly in a clear Italian-like blue sky. In the springtime it is even more impressive, as then, to the water from the glacier, are added masses of melting snow and blocks of ice from more than one lofty peak. The great blocks of ice go pounding over its rim to crash into the gorge below, and add more sound to the tremendous booming made by the falling water. I learned the value of seeing these natural phenomena at the proper season when in Texas some years ago. I had gone there to see the Rio Grande, and expected to behold a wondrous river, worthy of its grandiloquent name, but was disappointed to see a small sluggish stream meandering between wide mud-banks; but it was late summer and a dry season. Had I not revisited the river some time afterwards, in late spring this time in New Mexico, when the snow was still melting on the Rockies, I might have remembered Rio Grande as something of a misnomer. On my second visit the river was transformed and had turned into a raging torrent of water tearing madly down to the sea. It was then indeed a grand river.

The roar of Dettifoss, like Gullfoss, is heard long before the eye gazes on the magnificent scene, which is cunningly hidden from the visitor until he is close to it. Then the fall bursts upon the eye in a single moment and the sight is breath-taking. It gains charm from the fact that in addition to the main fall there are two smaller ones, caused by a deflection of the river bed and some intervening rocks.

Unlike Dettifoss, Gullfoss is non-glacial, and its waters are blue while those of Dettifoss have the peculiar milky colour common to glacier water because of the silt it carries. So great is the quantity of silt in all the glacial rivers of Iceland that it becomes easy to realise how tremendously the landscape must alter in the course of even a few generations, let alone a million years. It is quite possible to deposit on a gravel bed from a glacial river a layer of earth that will be food-producing in a few years, and Icelanders are actually using glacial deposit of this kind at Kirkjubæjarklaustur. At Dettifoss the quantity of silt is so great that one can see it separate from the water as it flows over the rim, streaking the milky water with long dark lines. This gives the fall a strange woolly appearance, and helps to make it one of the most pleasing in Europe.

Much of east Iceland is glacier country and everywhere there is evidence of the Ice-age which once gripped all the northern part of Europe. Long before reaching Dettifoss the white monstrous form of Vatnajökull, the greatest of the hangovers of the ice-age, is visible, lying like a recumbent giant between the mountain tops. No wonder these icy monsters cut vast valleys and deposit immense boulders all over the countryside. Their slow-moving mass contains so much weight that little can resist it, and so new topographical forms are cut out. The southern coast line of Iceland demonstrates this so clearly that it must be a veritable museum for geographers and siesmologists. With the aid of volcanoes, earthquakes and tearing winds, the coast line has been scarred and cut into edges—terrible but magnificent.

The gorge of Dettifoss is somewhat deceitful. No one can honestly deny it due praise for magnificence, but owing to the depth of the river bed, the water which streams through it from the fall is not impressive, and at the foot of the fall it is even unimpressive. Water, wind and time have cut the steep, rocky sides into numerous fantastic shapes, all of them impressive, and I rank it as among the finest of its kind that I have looked upon. One cannot, however, compare it to the wonderful Colorado gorge in Montana two thousand feet deep and wide, and still less with the Grand Canyon, Colorado. Doubtless time has had something to do with this, although no river in Iceland can be compared with the 1,500 miles that the Colorado River traverses from its source to the sea. Nor has the gorge at Dettifoss the same beauty of colour as those of the Colorado River. The gorges of the Colorado scintillate with every colour of the rainbow, but the basaltic and igneous rocks of Dettifoss lack the elements to reflect the colours of the sun. But when one compares the smallness of Iceland with the hugeness of America no apology is necessary.

Godafoss must be included in any serious consideration of Iceland's waterfalls, as it ranks in beauty if not in size with its two more famous competitors. It is the third largest of the island's waterfalls, and, lying on the main highway between Akureyri and Húsavík, is more often viewed. It was a dull day when I visited it and the absence of sun robbed it of some of its charm. It is so formed, however, that it can rely for its popularity on its shape without much regard to colour, and has the additional appeal of having some historical connections. Notable among these is an incident when a famous Icelander fell down a hole hidden from view.

Godafoss, although not so lofty or wide as Dettifoss and Gullfoss, reminds one of the latter because of the variety of its form. It consists of three separate bodies of water of different shapes and somewhat different elevations; and if one cares to include as a fourth fall the slender stream which drops with feathery consistency to the north of the main falls, and as a fifth the short fall down in the gorge, five would be the proper number. The largest of the three main bodies of water falls over the rim as a single column, weighty and very imposing; next to it at a slightly higher level, rushing madly between two large rocks comes the second fall; then comes the third column of water, so different in appearance from the others that one might be excused for suspecting that it had been purposely made by a clever designer. It breaks into no fewer than eight different falls, owing to the disposition of dark rocks; but they are so close together that they combine into a solid body of water before reaching the gorge below. The fourth fall is as good a contrast as one can imagine—all combining to create an unforgettable scene.

The water in the gorge is much more impressive than that at Dettifoss, although the quantity is much less; but the gorge at Dettifoss is vastly more imposing. The water in the gorge at Godafoss regains something of importance when compared to that at Dettifoss, for whereas the waters of the latter flow calmly away, those of Godafoss speed along, a raging, roaring torrent; a truly noble sight.

It is unnecessary to try to paint the particular features of Mulafoss, Gullfoss and still lesser lights; but like human families, what the bigger children may possess in bulk and strength, the smaller may make up in prettiness and neatness of outline. And just as each child makes a special appeal to the hearts of its parents, so do the waterfalls of Iceland appeal to Icelanders. Each, no matter how insignificant, has, like Iceland's mountains, been named, and is recalled with fondness.

CHAPTER 9

EAST BY PLANE

ICELAND has no railways, and never will have, unless one counts the few metres of railway that are found on the quay at Reykjavík. The best way to reach the east coast was therefor by airplane which does the journey of about 270 miles in three hours. This is a vast improvement upon the route by sea, which is about 100 miles longer and takes two days.

I was fortunate in having as my companion Mr. Sigbjorn Armann who is known as "the Salmon King," and who knows as much about his native land as any man living. It was he who planned the route and by his conversation enriched it beyond measure, as he seemed to know every nook and cranny of the country.

The airplane started on 12th July, after three days' delay because of bad weather. It is to be hoped that aviation may yet find means of defeating the weather clerk when he is in a bad mood, as there is much inconvenience occasioned by standing by for several days with travelling bags packed, unable to do anything in case a message comes from the airport that the trip can be made without delay.

It is impossible to reach the east coast by travelling along the south coast highway, owing to Vatnajökull. Hereabouts the mountains come right down to the sea's edge and nothing wider than a bridle path can be made through them. Even here, however, a few scattered farms exist, some of them in what looked from the plane to be almost inaccessible places. It was thought too that the plane would give me the best view of the southern coast, as well as enable me to see to greater advantage the three glaciers that lie in these parts.

It soon became apparent that a mistake had been made, and had I not, a few weeks later, traversed the South coast by car, almost up to the west side of Vatnajökull, I should have formed a very wrong idea of its topography as well as of its arable nature and the number of flourishing farms that line it. The plane flattened the country out, and furthermore, caused me, for some quite unaccountable reason, to believe that it was very sparsely populated, when the reverse is the truth. In a plane one perhaps moves too fast to make proper observation, and too much scenery engages the eye, with the consequence that as much is missed as is seen. But flying has its charms and enabled me to see the country from a different angle. The coast line is, of course, much plainer, and the view much more extensive.

Owing to the cloudy sky we flew at a low altitude, seldom rising higher than 800 feet instead of the usual 2,500 feet. The reason for this was to avoid having to descend from a mist which might have caused the plane to foul the mountain tops. The poor visibility made it difficult to see the glaciers, partly because the fog forced the pilot to keep well out to sea. Eyjafjallajökull andMýrdalsjökull were only just visible, but I was destined when motoring past them later to see them both close up and to advantage.Mýrdalsjökull is in a constant state of motion and it had already reached the level of the sea. The many rivers that flow from these glaciers were often clearly visible and some of them looked mighty fierce.

Vatnajökull came into sight while still a great distance off. I was destined to see this glacial monster on and off for several days as I moved about the east and north coasts of Iceland; and although I was unfortunately not able to approach to its borders, I met at least one man who had flown over it in a private plane. It had been my hope that the plane in which I travelled would have been able to take a similar route, but fate was against me.

There were, however, several interesting features which would have been missed had I not flown, one of them being a pirate trawler flying the British flag. Fishing piracy consists of fishing within three miles of the shore. The restriction is stringently imposed on all nations, including Icelanders, the object being to stop young fish from being netted in the spawning grounds. The penalties are very severe, including a fine of £1,000 and the confiscation of the entire catch and gear. One of the air plane crew laughingly informed me that the previous week, when flying very low, they passed over a British trawler that was pirating, and in its hurry to escape detection, cut its gear and made off. The passengers treated the whole matter as a huge joke, admitting that their own trawlers were often guilty of this offence; the loss of gear must have been very expensive and in itself a severe penalty.

From the air most of the south coast looks very uninviting, especially the long bleak-looking black volcanic beaches washed down by the glaciers. The outlook for shipwrecked sailors must be gloomy, and there are a good many shipwrecks on this coast; but a thoughtful country has made ample provision, erecting small huts along the shore to house the shipwrecked mariners. These pretty little buildings are quite conspicuous, being painted white with red roofs, and close to each is erected a tall pole, or signal post, to enable them to be located more easily in snowy weather. Some of these huts are placed at the openings of little inlets to shield them from the wind, and to make them more conspicuous they are sometimes erected on elevated ground.

One of the most conspicuous landmarks is Ingólfshöfdi, or "Ingolf's head," a small flat-topped rock on which Ingólfur Arnarson settled for one year on first arriving in Iceland. It must remain somewhat of a mystery, I think, why he selected this barren, unsheltered spot, and one wonders how he succeeded in surviving or where he procured his food. He appears, soon afterwards, to have moved farther west with his foster brother, Hjörleifur, and from his new home set out to find the main pillars of his house which were eventually washed ashore at Reykjavík. Hjörleifur decided to stay at Hjörleifshofdi, as unpromising and exposed a rock as Ingólfshöfdi, and here he was murdered by his Irish slaves, who decamped to the Westmen Islands, visible in the distant west. The murderers were sometime afterwards tracked down by Ingólfur and slaughtered.

From here the journey is supplied by an abundance of rugged, barren, and steep mountains, yet every now and then a prosperous farm appears. Each farm in Iceland is located and named on a good map as conspicuously as towns and villages in other countries. This is, cartographically, one of Iceland's peculiarities, and must please the farmers whose homes are thus historically perpetuated. When looking at a map of Iceland the uninitiated is sure to be misled into thinking it is well-filled with populous centres. There is one other peculiarity which seems to belie the smallness of its population; owing to the highways being necessarily reduced to a minimum, everybody travelling must use the same roadways, and one is then almost sure to meet some-one. The impression left on me was that I had never been in a country with so many people to so small a population! It certainly gives the impression that Iceland contains many more than 130,000 people.

Most of the eastern mountains were snow-capped, notwithstanding it being mid-summer and one of the warmest for, perhaps, fifty years. There must be something more than mere temperature that accounts for this. The close proximity of Vatnajökull partly explains it, and doubtless experts can account for the rest.

The sun came out and considerably changed the aspect of the scenery, especially the sea, which altered as if by magic from a leaden-grey to a lovely blue-green. The lower reaches of Vatnajökull now came into view. For some reason or other different parts of this vast glacier have been given different names, which makes it very confusing to the visitor. It has actually been divided into twelve subsidiary glaciers.

At this stage we caught sight of Papey, a group of islets on which some Roman Catholic priests settled long before Ingólfur arrived. Here too was shown an unaccountable preference for small almost inaccessible islands to the mainland. Probably it was due to fear lest the mainland was inhabited by a truculent race; or perhaps to a superstitious dread of elves, giants and devils who might object to the presence of strangers.

Shortly afterwards the plane turned abruptly into Fáskrúdsfjördur, to disembark some passengers and to take on fresh ones. The fjörd presented a very pretty scene with its prosperous-looking farms scattered along the sides of the mountains, all of which were streaked with snow, and down which ran numerous small cataracts. We were flying so low that it made some of the passengers sick with fright; but a low altitude was unavoidable owing to the narrowness of the fjörd. We were, however, to receive an even greater test of our nerves when, after leaving Budir, the little settlement at the end of the fjörd, we turned into Reydarfjördur, where my companion and I disembarked. Here the plane seemed almost to touch the side of the mountain, but smart handling by the pilot landed us safe and sound. Both fjörds are very lovely, especially Faskrudsfjördur. In Reydarfjördur we encountered a number of air-pockets which sent us every now and then careering downward at a speed more than our stomachs could stand.

From the huddle of small houses and Nissen huts which comprise Budareyri, at the far end of Reydarfjördur, to Egilstadir one gets a splendid idea of the beauty and richness of the eastern part of Iceland. The highway runs through a valley which presents, as do perhaps all other valley roads in Iceland, ever-changing scenes of a most pleasing kind. There is the inevitable river supplied by a hundred tiny waterfalls and cataracts, which sparkle in the sunshine and make the hills look alive. With the exception of one locality there is the usual absence of trees; but even this is compensated for by enabling the eye to watch the mysterious and grotesque variations of the mountains. Barren rock is relieved by patches of vivid green; for here as elsewhere the grass resembles that of Ireland more than that of England. Doubtless this is caused by the great amount of daylight summer brings to this land.

The "forest" makes quite an interesting break in the scenery, which is, of course, composed of rocky eminences, loose boulders, and rushing streams. Iceland has more than its fair share of boulders everywhere, especially around

Reykjavík; but whereas they are largely of lava structures there, in the east, they are composed of basalt and often of a rich brown colour.

Egilstadir is marked on maps fairly conspicuously and the stranger is surprised to find that it is nothing more than a large hostelry and a flourishing farm, situated on the shores of Lake Largarfljót. Well might the lucky Icelander who dwells in this part of the land cry proudly, "How green is my valley," owing to the lake feeding the soil with glacier water, and to the valley being shielded by mountains and hills from cold, destructive winds. The house-weary eyes of the city dweller cannot fail to feel delightfully rested when gazing on such a scene, and it again becomes evident why there are so many poets in Iceland. To the artist there is much to inspire and not a little to depress: how can any brush do justice to the mountainous scenery of this land! The cleverest brush can do little more than catch a fleeting moment of beauty, while actually the hills and valleys change with every sweep of the eye and movement of a cloud, wind and sun. The sensitive soul must despair in its utter impotency to describe such scenes. But Icelandic artists often catch the spirit, and their canvasses do not fail to please. Although they are almost invariably heavy and often quite oppressive.

Sunsets are among the principal glories of Iceland. I had seen many of these utterly entrancing scenes when in Reykjavík. As the sun sinks briefly below the horizon, which it does in summer with the exception of one day a year, it casts its rays on to heavens and clouds and produces such magnificent colour schemes that they must be seen to be even faintly appreciated.

At Egilstadir I was to see my first eastern sunset and shall never forget the night I spent seated on a hill-top watching the ever-changing sky. Many Icelanders make it a practice not to miss these marvels of beauty, and every night in town and country they may be seen watching the brilliant and sombre colours which fill the heavens. It is during the months of June, July and August that Old Sol produces his best effects. For several weeks, therefore, the lover of light and colour may feast at the heavenly banquet. Not even when heavy storm clouds fill the sky need one be disappointed, for the powerful rays of the sun will pierce wherever possible and produce a magical effect.

There are no limits to the shades of colour; and as the sun sinks slowly beneath horizon or behind the mountain peaks, the colours flare into full view. I have seen the distant heavens a deep burning red, gradually fading into orange, yellow, green, blue, indigo and violet, when the sky was free from clouds; but when clouds besprinkle the heavens, catching the rays of the sinking sun, they will split up into the colours of the spectrum in a most amazing way. In a sky heavy with dark clouds, too dense for the sun to penetrate, their edges will be lit with glory, and one may see here and there a thinning of the clouds penetrated by the sun's rays, while small clouds float like masses of living fire. They will even seem to burst and throw out long streamers of red light as if a mountain had suddenly exploded with volcanic fire.

The effects on the heavens as a whole, when seen without any impediment to check the eye, is to make it appear like an immense dome; the centre a deep blue, gradually changes into lighter hues as the gaze wanders in the direction of the setting sun, until it hurts through the brilliance of the colours. Let the eye sweep the encircling heavens until it rests upon the part most distance from the sun, and there the lighter edge will again appear, less bright, but no less charming. Every cloud that flecks the sky will contribute its quota of beauty to the breath-taking scene, in which burnished gold nearly always plays a part.

Now watch the mountains as their snow-capped peaks reflect the light which falls upon them; or, as sometimes they do, absorb it. A mist may enwrap the entire mass so that it appears to be covered by a mantle of purple or mauve; the snow, breaking the regularity of the scene, glowing as if a volcano were burning beneath it or as if crowned with a golden diadem. Occasionally a mountain peak will so catch the rays of the sun that it will appear like an immense fire, while the snow on its peak and sides will be broken by dark boulders and bluffs from which the snow has melted.

Added to all this is the valley which lies stretched out before the charmed eye. This too, is a study in colour and form, both where nature persists unadorned and where the hand of man has added enchantment. Perhaps upon a slight eminence or partly hidden from view in a desultory hollow, stands a modern or an ancient farm. The former built of concrete with straight, plain, unornamented walls and numerous windows inset with small panes of glass, its white walls being offset by a bright red or green roof; the latter with its stone and turf walls and grass-green roof. Nearby may be barns and stalls equally modern, or perhaps intermixed with older stone and earth erections that have long withstood the test of time, all revealing the prosperity and progress of the farmer.

Scattered over the valley or on the mountainside will be numerous sheep, left throughout the season to fend for themselves; but hours ago the cows came home to be milked and herded in their sheds. Farms are distributed throughout the valley, and give a comfortable air of neighbourly companionship. In the foreground lies the lake, shining like silver even at this late hour in the reflected rays of the sinking sun, while the brilliantly-coloured clouds are reflected less clearly in the milky glacial waters. Here and there a red glint moves lazily on the water's edge, as the red-gold of some particularly brilliant cloud strikes upon it.

The presence of the sea often enhances these celestial glories, especially on the northern coast. I have been privileged to see the sunset on a thousand hills in countries scattered about the globe, but none have equalled the sunsets of Iceland. It is literally true to say that here mountains may assume any colour, because of the remarkable effect of the sun upon the light mists which in the evening so often enshroud them.

Egilstadir may be taken as one of the best examples of an Iceland guesthouse, having also some of its defects. I have never been in an Icelandic guest house that had carpets on the floors or wardrobes in the bedrooms. But Egilstadir did have wall pegs on which one could hang clothes. All the others without exception were deficient more or less in even these; and since as a rule they lodge two or more persons in a room this is a definite inconvenience. It is strange that a people who are both polite and considerate by nature should lack these necessaries, for it does one's garments no good to be left unceremoniously on the floor, or doubtfully on an already over-filled chair. There was, of course, no great reason for me to complain as I seldom stayed more than one or two nights; but to those who remain for longer periods it must be a serious discomfort.

At Egilstadir the food was excellent, and Iceland lacks no food. Among the distressed countries of Europe this island can load its tables with ample supplies. On my arrival at the hostelry I was served with an evening meal, the main dish consisting of what I mistook for eggs and bacon, but which turned out to be smoked mutton, a favourite dish in Iceland. Not only did it look like gammon of bacon, but it tasted like it. It was served with fried eggs, green peas, potatoes, rye and white bread and butter, black pudding made of sheep's blood mixed with the fat of kidneys; cheese, raw fish and tea or coffee, with the almost inevitable glass of milk. One peculiarity of Iceland is soups. These are often made with fruits, which Britons as a rule reserve for dessert; prune, apricot and raisin soups being common. Green foods are always conspicuous by their absence. During my brief stay at Egilstadir many holiday-makers came and went, including large char-a-banc parties, because Egilstadir was on the main highway between the north and the east. Most visitors dined together at long tables, small tables being introduced merely to fill up odd corners of the dining-room; and it mattered not whether the diners were together or not, they shared willingly the same table, on which the delicious viands were placed *en masse*, the diners helping themselves and courteously passing the dishes round.

This communal mode of dining has its advantages, as

Icelanders, unlike most other people, do not act as strangers to each other and are not shy towards each other, although they present a reserve to foreigners. In my case this restraint was not very conspicuous partly because of my readiness to start conversations, and partly because the news had gone round that I intended writing a book about the country. This opened many a mouth and produced many interesting anecdotes and scraps of information, as all Icelanders take pride in their national literature, and are especially interested in anything pertaining to their native land. Even the proprietor invited me to dine with him and two or three of his friends, all of whom could speak English and were well-informed.

Icelanders resemble Americans in their willingness to talk about their native land, and most of them are intimately acquainted with its history. This I imagine presents no difficulty, as Iceland has, ever since its discovery, been free from most of those international complications that harass larger countries. After being annexed by Denmark, Iceland may be said to have settled down definitely to a domestic policy, unfortunate and unpleasant as it may, in the earlier days have been.

For the most part their history seems to have been chiefly connected with farm-life and fishing, Denmark for a long time having taken care of everything else. The consequences have not been very good for Iceland which, until its complete separation from Denmark in 1941, paid far too little attention to its national institutions and relics, but has since tried to make amends. It is now doing its utmost to collect for the National Museum in Reykjavík everything that will throw light on the past. Up to now the results have been rather poor, as a visit to the Museum reveals, but the Government has now become so history-conscious that everything, no matter how slight it may be, that has real traditional value is being collected and catalogued.

Owing to this willingness to talk and the frequency with which English is spoken, Britishers and Americans are at no great disadvantage in collecting information. At Egilstadir, for instance, at least one third of the visitors spoke English fairly well, especially those who earned their living on the sea. There arrived while I was there a party of trawler captains with their families, and all of the men spoke excellent English and were acquainted with England.

While at this guest-house I made a journey to Seydisfjördur, a pretty little seaside town over the worst highway in Iceland. It ran over the summit of a lofty range of mountains and demonstrated something of the immense difficulties travellers must face when travelling this route in winter. But the inconvenience of the highway was well compensated for the by magnificent scenery; and when descending the mountains on the east side, I do not recall seeing anything in the entire country more bewitching. Right at the highest part of the mountain stood a ramshackle Saeluhús, or rest house, for the protection of wayfarers compelled to take shelter from the elements or to rest and recuperate. It contained the necessary equipment of oil-stove, lamp, fuel, table and chairs; but as the windows were broken and the door open through a defective lock, it would have ill-served its purpose at that time. These rest houses are to be found on other dangerous routes, for travelling over mountains in winter must be very precarious.

Dangerous as the road was, motor lorries and 'buses negotiate it whenever possible, and the authorities are making a new highway which may not be completed, for Seydisfjördur is losing its former significance and there is a possibility of its being finally abandoned through the failure of its fishing facilities. Two features may, however, rescue the road from utter decay. One is the magnificence of the mountain scenery as one descends to Seydisfjördur; the other, Mulafoss and Gufufoss, two of Iceland's most alluring waterfalls, both of which lie along the route. The first view of Seydisfjördur from the top of the mountain is entrancing. No prettier scene of its kind is to be found anywhere. Seydisfjördur is dying very charmingly as it nestles cosily at the foot of the mountain at the end of the fjörd. The better road to Reydarfjördur, as well as the absence of herring at Seydisfjördur seems to have sounded the death knell of the latter, as trade is taking the line of least resistance and is already largely diverted to the former town.

Perturbing as the trip to Seydisfjördur had been, a still more exciting and hazardous one took me from Egilstadir to Vidfjördur, a small fjord forming a branch of the better-known Nordfjördur. It is doubtful whether in all my foreign travels I had experienced anything quite so adventurous as this. For the main part the highway was little more than a dirt track, constructed out of loose stones from the mountain-side. From Eskifjördur it ran for several miles perilously along the edge of the mountains composing the north side of the fjörd, and then took a tortuous pathway over a mountain crest.

We did the trip of twenty-five miles late at night in weather dull enough to necessitate headlights, which in all probability made the highway look worse than it really was. The fact that at two o'clock the following morning Mr. Armann and I arrived safely at our destination, spoke volumes for the skill and nerve of the driver. Few private cars seemed to attempt this journey, and on the way we met more than one that had been abandoned by its owner, who evidently concluded that prudence was the better part of valour.

Motor 'buses in Iceland take the place of trains elsewhere, and are a favoured mode of transportation by these descendants of the old Vikings, much of whose intrepidity was exhibited by the passengers who appeared quite impervious to their danger. During this journey the 'bus crossed no fewer than thirty-four water-courses mostly without bridges, because of the shallow water; they would remain without them, for the Government had decided to make a new road with a slightly different course, which accounted, I found, for the obvious neglect of this one. It is amazing to learn that this highway had been negotiated by motor 'buses for thirty years without a serious accident! The 'bus on which I travelled contained twenty-six passengers on the outward journey, and about six extra passengers when two days later I reluctantly returned over the same route.

This was in daylight and I was better able to see the dangers of the previous journey, as the highway ran for a considerable distance along a lofty mountain ridge, to fall over which would have plunged the vehicle several hundred feet into a valley below, in which ran more than one stream ready to finish off anyone whom the fall may have left alive.

CHAPTER 10

THE HAUNTED FARM

IT was with a sigh of relief that my companion and I alighted at the isolated farmhouse where we had planned to stay a few days. Vidfjördur is one of the almost forgotten fjörds. Like Seydisfjördur, its fortune changed when the herring deserted it, as cod, halibut, and other varieties of fish follow herring, on which they live. The cause of this desertion is not known. It is thought that it may have been due to an alteration of the Gulf Stream, which at one time flowed into the fjörd, but has been diverted by arctic currents. Herring, preferring the warm water, have followed the Stream.

Vidfjördur is one of the most sparsely-populated of the east coast fjörds, containing only four farms, three on the east side and one on the west, the fjörd turning southward. It was the one on the western shore that we visited—a large, three-storey, plain building, painted white according to the all-prevailing custom. One interesting feature about this farm is that it is renowned for being haunted.

The three days I spent with this delightful household afforded me an excellent insight into the way in which old Icelanders lived; for, with the exception of a radio and a telephone, the family were compelled to live the same kind of life as their ancestors. The present house is only twelve years old, but has many of the deficiencies of the older farm, on the foundations of which it has been erected. They draw their water from a well, and have absolutely no sanitary arrangements.

The interior of the house shows clearly that no skilled architect designed it and no highly qualified builder constructed it, the staircases having been put in, apparently, as an afterthought. The furnishings are in strict keeping with the building in general, and are plain to the point of severity. No carpets cover the floors, and most of the walls are distempered. The chairs are crude wooden ones, almost all devoid of upholstery.

The old-fashioned wooden bedsteads are the same kind as those used in every Icelandic farm a century ago. Some of the chairs and tables are home-made, also a quaint old desk which shows clearly that the dead hand which constructed it had other qualifications than that of a fisherman and farmer.

The farm is practically cut off from the outside world, being three-quarters of an hour's sea voyage to Nordfjördur, the nearest town one way, and several hours' pony ride over the mountain, the other. Furthermore, they are unable to reach any of the other three farms in the fjörd except by pony along a narrow track, half way up what looks like an inaccessible cliff. It is, therefore, not difficult to realise how restricted are their resources for pleasure. The pony track to the other farms is not more than twelve inches wide and in winter time very difficult to negotiate. Thus they are often cut off from their neighbours even more than from Nordfjördur round the end of the fjörd. It is to this town that they must go for anything other than potatoes, milk, eggs and meat. These they supply themselves from their farm. There is plenty of poultry, but they are used only for producing eggs, as, in common with many Icelanders, they have a rooted objection to eating birds, why, I have never been able to discover. When the birds die their carcasses are usually thrown away. Icelanders are noted bird lovers and strongly object to their destruction, a fact which they soon make plain to the visitor from abroad.

Nevertheless, they were a well-dressed, healthy, well-fed family, the four children comparing more than favourably with the children of townsfolk. These children ranging in age from three to fifteen years were apparently perfectly satisfied with life, and seemed to find no drawback in their restricted environment. The radio appealed to them as much as to their elders, and in the evening they would sit round the receiving set listening attentatively to good music.

A more agreeable family it would have been difficult to find. Not one cross word or look escaped them while I was there, and everyone seemed to fit perfectly into the general harmony of the home. In common with Icelanders their manners were the best possible, and one could see they were naturally polite and well-behaved although by no means self-conscious. No one would have suspected that the fifteen-year-old boy and his step-father were employed in road-making because the farm was slack; the field work being done by the four women, ranging in age from twenty-seven to eighty years.

The family never attended church owing to the nearest one being at Nordfjördur, boats sailing there only three times a week. But they faithfully listen in to the Sunday service on the radio, their favourite preachers being two clergymen known for their modern views. Both of these clergymen are members of the Icelandic Society for Psychical Research and are, therefore, not 'Old-fashioned.'

Doubtless these charming people still favour something of the old Viking faith and have a good deal of respect for the shades of their departed ancestors; a not uncommon feeling among these islanders. Tragedy has stalked this household which, having in the past wrung its livelihood from the sea, has paid a heavy price. A few years ago three of the old lady's sons were drowned in the same trawler and three other members of the family have lost their sweethearts in the same tragic manner, one having lost two. In this way, different members of the family have died for generations, and only now that the herring have departed from the fjörd has this cause of death ceased to threaten them from day to day.

I have recounted the history of this family somewhat fully because many features connected with it illustrate the kind of life that Icelanders lived in the past. Deaths by sea are responsible to a great extent for the smallness of Iceland's population, and as long as fishing remains its principal industry, this bitter toll must be paid. Some of the vessels in which they go to sea are pitiably small, many frail

7. *The Mountain Essa seen from Reykjavík.*

8. *Evening in Iceland during the Midnight Sun*

and old. Fishermen themselves are readily prepared to admit this. Now that Iceland is more prosperous it will be possible to build larger and safer vessels, and thus rob death of a good deal of its sting.

Any English farmer might well smile at the farming of this Icelandic family. Practically nothing was visible to show that it cultivated anything, except perhaps the four fine husky sheep dogs that lay so patiently outside the doorway watching it with pensive gaze. Like the people in the house they were among the friendliest of creatures, and revealed by their presence that there must be sheep somewhere. I found some of them as I strolled gingerly along the side of the fjörd and met no human being. The end of the fjörd was about two miles away, but throughout the whole of that walk I saw no more than four sheep and as many lambs wandering among the numerous boulders of granite-like rock, apparently eating seaweed. There must, of course, have been many more somewhere on the mountain, but none for the moment was in view.

The wind was boisterous, thrashing the waters of the fjörd into flecked fury; and as the waves beat against the steep shores, foam and spray were flung high into the air. It was night time and the sun was sinking, its declining rays topping the mountains on the side of the fjörd turning the rich brown rock of which they were composed into burnished gold. Here, surely, was a place to inspire anyone. It is no wonder that the father of the present owner of the farm was something of a poet, and loved literature more than he loved farming; leaving behind a record of his consummate penmanship in an old wood-covered book which he bound himself and lovingly encased in a crude box also made by himself.

It is difficult to judge the economic conditions of such a family as this one, unless one knows how many sheep and cattle they have. It was obvious from the small patches of cultivated land, scattered here and there, that what vegetables they grew were for their own consumption. During the last fifty years there has taken place a great increase in the value of sheep and cows. Whereas formerly a sheep cost only six kronur, today it would cost at least 200 kronur, an advance greater than the general cost of living. The same ratio of increase applies to kine; and the farmer who has a considerable number of sheep and a large herd of kine is very well off. But, on the whole, farming in Iceland is said not to be profitable, the main reason for this being the high cost of labour. This little farm employed no one, and being self-contained, was doubtless prosperous, especially as its inhabitants had little taste for luxuries.

In my honour they served at mid-day on Sunday their best and most luxurious dish. It consisted of boiled lambs' heads, a dozen of which lay pathetically on the large dish in the centre of the table. If these tiny creatures had been killed expressly for me, the meal must have been costly, and I cannot say that I enjoyed it very much.

CHAPTER 11

AFFORESTATION

UNDOUBTEDLY one of the most peculiar features of Iceland is the dearth of trees, and Icelanders feel it keenly. They regard it with a feeling akin to shame. However, they derive some consolation in the fact that the Sagas insist that at one time the country was covered with forests, and the quantity of peat which is continually dug up affords conclusive proof. It is no uncommon thing to see huge piles of this bogwood carefully packed up drying for winter use.

From the earliest times visitors to the island noticed this deficiency of trees, and drew attention to it. It is still one of the things that immediately attract the attention of the foreigners, and several British and American soldiers commented on it to me.

At first one is inclined to attribute it to the nature of the soil, for the unpropitious-looking lava and igneous rock and boulders that meet the eye on the outskirts of Reykjavík seem to justify this conclusion. But much of the country round Reykjavík is by no means representative of the entire country. The eastern, northern and southern parts of the island have large areas free from both types of soil and substance. Furthermore, lava is quite good for certain trees, and it soon becomes apparent that most of the so-called forests of Iceland grow among lava beds. Few of the trees grow beyond the sapling size, however, and one is, therefore, inclined to believe that this is due to fire having destroyed nourishing elements.

Icelanders try to cover their confusion in this matter by assuring the visitor that somewhere out east or up north are to be found trees at least thirty feet tall; but whoever goes in search of them may feel inclined to attribute this statement to imagination. At Akureyri the statement becomes justified, not in the open country, however, for there the trees are mere bushes, but to some extent in the pretty little park that has been established by the nature-loving women of that attractive town, while a visit to the Nursery which nestles at the foot of the cliffs on the west side of the fjörd fully justifies the claim.

Here the eye is at last gladdened by the sight of a small wood of fairly tall trees, some of which reach perhaps to thirty-five or forty feet. It is obvious, therefore, that trees can grow in Iceland, but they require close and skilled attention. The Government has decided to make good this deficiency and has established an afforestation farm at Hallormsstadur, on the shores of Largarfljót, a lake which has the peculiarity of being merely a widening of a river flowing from Vatnajökull. This location has doubtless been chosen because in it is to be found the largest natural forest in Iceland.

I was motored to the afforestation farm from Egilstadir, and the forest but confirmed my earlier conclusion that trees will not easily grow here, for, although it extends several miles along the shores of the lake and is at least half a mile wide, none of the trees reach thirty feet. This, notwithstanding Skogarvellir, the district in which the forest is situated, being among the most arable in the country.

Not one of these trees was tall enough or straight enough to be of much commercial use, and could serve no purpose other than to supply fire-wood, wind-breaks, or decorations. Icelandic trees have curiously contorted trunks, which make them attractive to the eye; but that is not good enough, even for optimistic Icelanders. It is singular that Iceland's trees should be so tenuous and twisted, as they fit well into the general landscape in which they generally grow.

The afforestation farm is expertly conducted, the young shoots growing in orderly array according to their age. It takes three years to make them strong enough to stand the strain of transplantation; the first year being spent entirely under cover, as the strength of the sun is more than they can bear. Several kinds of trees are cultivated including birch, beech, yew, larch and various kinds of pine, some of which have been imported from climates suitable to trees in Iceland.

It will, of course, take a good many years before the experiment can prove its worth, but in the meantime farmers are patronising the scheme wholeheartedly, as they need trees for, among other purposes, that of beautifying their property, shielding their land from the ravages of wind and for the atmospheric changes growing trees afford.

The cause of the denudation of Iceland of its trees is well-known and quite obvious. The island is practically without coal; Iceland must, therefore, turn to the importation of this necessity, at great expense. In the early days, therefore, before importation of coal was possible and electricity to convey water to town and farms from natural hot springs unknown, wood and peat were the sole means of heating dwellings. In the course of a thousand years nearly every tree of useful size was cut down, used, or burned; and when trees commenced to grow, sheep ate the young shoots. Care is now taken to obviate this danger, and wherever trees grow on or near farms and cattle runs they are carefully guarded by fences.

Only one other part of the world where cultivation prevails have I seen as poorly stocked with trees as Iceland—Saskatchewan, Canada. Whoever has traversed this extensive territory must have felt the same depression that afflicted me as I gazed upon its rolling prairies, devoid of trees except where a thoughtful Government had planted "wind-breaks" on farms to shield them from driving wind and snow. But for these trees many of the farms of Saskatchewan would be covered with snow throughout the bitter winter months and life rendered unendurable.

Nowadays trees are absolutely necessary to man, not only to provide shelter, but for a host of other things, and to prevent soil erosion. America and Australia have taught the world a lesson in soil erosion through lack of trees, and many farmers have been ruined by the surface soil of their farms being blown away. I have seen this tragic process in

Nebraska, U.S.A., where heart-broken farmers watched the day darkened by clouds of good earth being pitilessly wafted away.

Previous to the introduction of concrete for house building, the later generations of Icelanders relied largely upon wood for the erection of homes. When they had used up the forests of the country, they imported it in quantities that must have contributed to the great poverty which afflicted them until comparatively recent times.

Man's progress has always been linked up with timber. Not only did it enable him to make a fire and thereby improve his diet, but he used it to build houses, to make furniture and ships; the last playing a very important part in the life of Iceland. Timber too made the plough that cultivated the field, and the flail that threshed the corn. In modern times metal has displaced these wooden implements, but war has plainly taught us that it is still very essential to man's defence and progress. Thriving agriculture has always been closely bound up with forests, and in all probability the restricted nature of Icelandic farming may be traced partly to the absence of trees. It is a remarkable fact that the chief product of Iceland's farms is hay, large tracts of land being devoted solely to this feed for cattle and sheep during the winter months. Relatively few vegetables are cultivated, potatoes being well in the ascendant, while turnips, carrots, tomatoes, rhubarb and one or two other vegetables in small quantities are also grown. Cabbages and other green foods are so rare that the vitamins which they supply have to be purchased from the pharmaceutical chemists.

Yet I have never met an Icelandic farmer who did not insist that vegetables of all kinds could be grown if they only took the trouble; but since they never do, one may be excused from being sceptical. Some corn can be cultivated, but wheat cannot, although many Icelanders insist that it can. It is doubtful if one acre is to be found in the whole country devoted to wheat. Probably the best answer to this desideratum is also lack of trees; and one factor which seems in favour of this is that flowers grow in profusion under cultivation, and for colour and size are able to hold their own with those of more temperate climes. The flowers of Iceland are on the whole more colourful than elsewhere. It is, indeed, admitted that one of the reasons why vegetables fare indifferently is owing to wind and frost, both of which could be greatly modified if there were sufficient trees.

With the development of Iceland's new afforestation scheme may take place a revolution in its second most important industry—farming. There is ample historic proof to guarantee this optimism, and with this development, Iceland may succeed in overcoming to a great extent her present economic insecurity. A country that relies upon one industry for its exports, is in a parlous state. Should fish cease to be required by foreign countries, Iceland will find herself in a sorry position, and she is alive to the fact. The present extraordinary prosperity is due almost entirely to the sale of fish and fish oil, and for the moment it is impossible to see what substitute can be found for them. Already she has had important lessons on the danger of fish desertion, several towns on the eastern and northern coasts being more or less doomed because herring have deserted their fjörds.

I spent a somewhat mournful afternoon in Seydisfjördur and had ample evidence of the sad situation. My companion, Mr. Sigbjorn Armann, had been born in Seydisfjördur and took me to see the house in which he had first seen daylight. It was on the west side of the fjörd and almost without exception the houses were empty, the inhabitants having been driven away by sheer necessity. No fish living! In my friend's boyhood days fishing had flourished and so did the town.

This phenomenon is not common to Iceland, although as a national danger it probably exists nowhere else to the same extent. Australia, New Zealand and America afford examples in connection with gold-mining, there being scattered about them the remains of towns and villages which flourished while the gold lasted; but as soon as the lodes ran out the settlement died and the population moved elsewhere. Some of these towns have excellent houses, revealing how prosperous they had been in their hey-day; but now not a solitary footstep echoes through the silent streets. But New Zealand, Australia and America do not depend wholly on gold.

In addition to the forest at Skogarvellir, there are three others which are more or less the pride of local residents. One is between Budareyri and Egilstadir, and another just outside Húsavík, and grows in a scattered kind of way among lava boulders. It extends more than a mile and a half and is fairly deep, and I do not think any of the "trees" stand over nine feet in height. They look bizarre, these trees growing amid lava, and lending colour to an otherwise dun scenery. It must be left to arboriculturists to explain how any form of life can derive nourishment from this firebaked earth and rock. Nearby the forest is the river Laxá, and in the distance can be seen Laxáfoss, a waterfall from which Akureyri, some forty miles away, receives power for its electricity.

A few kilometres further westward is Vaglaskogur, on the banks of the Fnjóska, of which Akureyri is particularly proud. It is composed entirely of birch trees, and large numbers of holiday makers wend their way thither to see this, to them, splendid "forest." The appeal to one who had seen the giant-like trees of New Zealand, Australia, Canada and the United States, is not the trees but their wonderful setting. The Fnjóska here takes a remarkable course, and viewed from the surrounding mountains up which the highway runs, it challenges comparison for beauty with many a more famous stream. It can be said for Iceland that whatever be the deficiencies of its forests or woods, they certainly have surroundings which must be the delight of artists, and will always be a source of joy to those privileged to visit them.

A short distance from Húsavík there is a remarkable rock formation, famous because of its extremely unusual nature and known as the "Castle of the Gods." It is an excellent example of the tricks nature can play with the surface of the earth through volcanic action. It consists of a huge rent leaving high cliffs standing like the walls of a mighty castle, the part torn away standing a short distance off like a land island. One hears strange stories about this grim but pleasing scene, which might well cause the sceptic to drop his scepticism and believe in nature spirits, for this would be a fitting abode for them. The hard magnificence of the place is softened by the pretty little wood which grows at the foot of the lofty cliffs, lending shade to the visitor who seeks for it after passing for so long across barren country. Small as this wood is, it counts considerably in an almost treeless land for, frequent as may be these clumps of trees, if they were all congregated in one spot they would not make more than a fair-sized forest.

Let us hope that in course of time Iceland will be able to add to its other attractions forests worthy of the other immensities of this island. It is a land of giants, and calls for equality in all aspects of nature. Icelanders rest content enough that one day the condition mentioned in the sagas will be restored, and a land, no longer driven by necessity to destroy much of its beauty and needful arborial inhabitants, will have the fine forests that her people long for and dream about.

CHAPTER 12

EAST TO NORTH

I TRAVELLED extensively about the East before going north to Húsavík, and found the country as beautiful and attractive as I had been led to believe it to be when in Reykjavík. Indeed, it appealed to me more than did the west and south coast, fascinating as they are.

Compared with the Rocky mountains, the Swiss and New Zealand Alps, the mountains of Iceland are in some ways more pleasing, largely because they are not so lofty and therefore more comprehensive. They are not so widely separated as the ranges of the Rockies, which are often divided by plains so extensive that one range disappears before the next comes into view. In Iceland one never loses sight of mountains, and in that respect it is almost unique. Many of the elevations are clearly defined and all of them have names which, like the mountains, can never be confused. Because of this definiteness every mountain has a distinct personality, and is apparently viewed in that way by the natives. Esja, Hekla, Akrafjall and Snaefell, for example, are so unalike that they are as individualistic as George Washington and Simon Bolivar.

The visitor soon grows to feel with Icelanders something of this personification of these mighty hills, and a kind of sympathy develops which makes one almost believe that each mountain lives. Perhaps most of us are animists at heart. The mountains vary greatly in colour too. To describe this to the uninitiated must seem merely an excess of imagination; but the fact remains that some of these mountains are red, some white, some heliotrope and some even dead black. I have more than once seen mountains standing out conspicuously because they were green or yellow or violet, and sometimes a veritable combination of brilliant colours. They change like a panorama when the sunlight plays upon them. Then, like many of the sheep that graze upon them, they may even appear to be piebald. I must confess to having been more affected by these Icelandic mountain scenes than by most other things during my stay, and in no other country was I so emotionally stirred.

To see a reddish mountain suddenly light up as if aflame simply because the rays of the sun shone upon it, seems to be a natural miracle. There is also a titanic effect about some of the isolated mountains like Herdubreid, Askja and Hengith. Each stands complete in itself, perfectly defined and personified. Such elevations may well be classed as aristocrats among Iceland's mountains. They are magnificent and this is enhanced by the fact that one can move round them from a distance, and see them change with every alteration of position. I travelled slowly round Herdubreid for the best part of a day, although the car in which I sat moved fast, and he presented a hundred different facets and all were intriguing. A similar statement can be made of numerous other mountains that grace the island's landscapes.

On the way to Dettifoss the car passed through the "Valley of Hell," a deep, long depression between raw mountains with hardly a blade of grass upon them. This valley earned its name partly because of its aridity and partly because of the danger of traversing it in winter. Heavy snowfalls then make it impossible for cars to pass through and ponies must be used. Even these sturdy little creatures often succumb to the hardships of the valley. Yet man has run through it long lines of telegraph and telephone poles which pass when necessary right over the mountain tops, speaking volumes for the intrepidity of Icelandic engineers in their determination to link up every part of the country, no matter how remote it may be. It must be remembered that only a small proportion of Iceland is inhabited and owing to the mountainous nature of the country, towns, villages and farms are often very wide apart; because of this the quickest way is often the longest, which, of course, does not help to ease the expense of making communications.

It is amazing how successful the Government has been in installing the telegraph and telephone. Its intention is to connect up every farm and private subscriber by these means within the next ten years, and to ensure speedy communications. I watched the workmen cutting channels for a trunk line from Reykjavík to Akureyri, a distance of 400 km. This meant conquering nature with a vengeance, and overcoming mountains, valleys and streams. The task was doubly hard and expensive because in laying the cable over numerous mountain tops the soft earth was often only a few inches deep and sometimes entirely absent, and channels had to be cut in the stone. The undertaking is like that of no other country in the world, for, apart from cutting through stone, the cable had to be run through lava fields, and glacial rivers, which, when in spate, roared and raged along. Furthermore, owing to the importance of sea communications with their fishing fleet, it is hoped that in the same period every vessel over ten tons will be equipped with a radio-telephone.

The boon telephones alone confer on Icelandic farmers is incalculable. Imagine a farm situated in a valley among almost inaccessible mountains, which effectively cut the inhabitants off from their nearest neighbour. To reach the next farm means travelling along a narrow pony track, here bordering a raging torrent, there passing over the very brow of a high hill. Such a journey, as I only too well saw, would be difficult enough in summer, and must be well-nigh impossible in winter when the snow covers everything, hiding the pony track and, when falling, obscuring the view. In the old days some farmers were cut off entirely from all outside communication. Today, even if they cannot reach each other in person, they can at least talk over the telephone; and in the hour of dire necessity attempts can be made to reach them and bring succour.

Mr. Helgi Sigurdsson, Chief Engineer of the State Telephones, and his deputy, Mr. Frithbjörn Adalsteinsson, informed me that the installing of telephones dates back to

1905, when the Marconi Company approached the Government with a view to the adoption of radio, and the first installation was established that year. From that time there has been a gradual improvement and extension of the system, and in 1938, there took place direct radio short-wave telegraphic communication with New York. Previous to that time all messages had to be relayed through London, England. The first submarine telegraph to London was laid in 1906.

The system in use throughout Iceland is automatic and it works extremely well, and one can be sure of getting speedy connections with other subscribers. Trunk lines, however, at present necessitate passing by automatic dialling to the exchange whence the call is relayed to the distant town. Steps are, however, being taken to dispense with this cumbersome method, and that is why the line is being laid between Reykjavík and Akureyri, through underground cables, for up till now lines have run overhead in conjunction with telegraphs.

It is difficult to see how this can be replaced by the safer underground method, as it requires much expense and labour to cut through solid rock. The present enterprise is the first attempt to link up the two largest towns. The line to Akureyri was started in 1939, and it is hoped that it will be finished by 1949, the principal difficulty being labour. The expense is high, but so essential is this undertaking to the proper development of the country that it is being faced. The cost works out somewhere in the region of 7,000 kronur for each kilometre; but notwithstanding that, the cost to subscribers is relatively low, although, owing to the alteration in money values, which is estimated at about three times of that before 1939, readjustment in charges must be made. It will then work out at somewhat less than in Britain with a population of nearly 50,000,000. Mr. Adalsteinsson invited me to talk to London by telephone, and the connection was made in a few minutes, the voice being perfectly clear.

There was a good deal of road-making going on, for the

construction of highways has become a necessity in these days of the automobile. Every now and then we would see lines of pretty white tents showing where the road-making gang were billeted; for road-makers in Iceland must often leave their homes for long periods. I knew two road-makers in the east and they reached home on Saturdays only to leave again Sunday night to walk many miles to their particular station, where they lived on the mountain top in tents.

The absence of railways and navigable rivers makes roads of great importance in Iceland, and some notable work has been done during the last few years in road construction. More than 3,000 miles of gravel roadways have been made, the main highways being in some instances exceptionally good. The country is now honeycombed with roadways and highways, some constructed and maintained by the Government, some by county authorities and others by municipalities.

An army of no fewer than two thousand workers are regularly employed on making and maintaining them, involving an annual expenditure of between £800,000 and £1,000,000. This represents 14 per cent. of the total national income! A tremendous sum for so small a population. These roadways, I found, were very serviceable, and wherever necessary they were built up, in some instances, as much as thirty feet, to ensure comfort and security and for keeping them free from snow. By being built up, the snow is blown off by the wind which is very prevalent most of the year.

These roads and highways vary from eight to fifteen feet in width, the latter figure applying to all main highways, which are, for the most part, made of gravel and lava. Few highways are asphalt or concrete, although two or three roads running out of Reykjavík are for a few kilometres.

Telegraph poles do not necessarily keep to the highways, but run over open country or mountains if that is the shorter way. Distance is very important, because every pole has to be imported. In consequence one sees telegraph poles running through almost impassable places, and cunning devices have been adopted to ensure their stability over terrain, the surface of which has proved too stubborn to be penetrated.

The pole must then be supported by other means. Usually piles of stones are placed round it, and judging from my observations none had fallen, even over extensive lava deposits.

Húsavík is the oldest settlement in Iceland. I entered it on the 16th July, with the sun shining brilliantly and the quaint little town looking peaceful and primitive. Although of recent growth in an important sense, Húsavík is without one conspicuous building, and as far as I could see, without one paved street. This primitiveness gives it much of its charm, for I must confess to having felt while there a certain tranquility and "far from the madding crowd."

It was here that the first settler arrived and made his temporary home. Not caring for the country, which he found cold and unpropitious owing to a severe winter, he departed and left to Ingólfur Arnarson the honour and fame of becoming the real originator of the nation.

Fifty years ago Húsavík was nothing more than a collection of farms and the homes of a few fishermen; a scattered parish extending to the arctic circle, including also a good deal of territory south of the town, all presided over by a Lutheran priest, who also farmed. Now fishing has become the principal industry, and Húsavík the third largest town in Iceland, with a population—including the entire district—of less than thirteen hundred souls.

The harbour is pretty and it was here that I got my first real insight into the dangers faced by Iceland's fishermen. In the harbour were several small fishing smacks, making the landsman wonder what chance such frail vessels would stand in a storm in this northern sea. I had a chat with two handsome young blond fishermen on one of the smallest of the smacks, moored to the jetty, and they expressed their dissatisfaction at the smallness of their craft, stating that such boats ought to be scrapped in favour of larger and more seaworthy vessels. Not only were the smacks often too small, they said, but many of them were too old; and the risk of sailing them considerable. They agreed that the Government had done wisely in taking a hand in the matter, for private enterprise, largely because of financial difficulties, had proved incapable of doing justice to both fishing and fishermen.

From the earliest days fishing had been of the greatest importance to Iceland, and from the fourteenth century has been its principal export. In the early days the fish in the fjörds has been one of the main assets of the country, and seem always to have constituted a principal item of national diet. Now, however, fishermen ventured far beyond the precincts of fjörd into the open sea where much rougher weather can be encountered, and larger and better boats are required. During the nineteenth century with its national depression a definite decline took place in the fisheries, but it eventually regained its former supremacy and looks like never losing it.

The history of the Icelandic fishing fleet is illuminating and interesting. Eighty years ago it consisted entirely of rowing boats, and in 1876 no fewer than 3,280 were employed. The work was then terribly dangerous and the death toll heavy enough to account for the slow growth of population, due allowance being made for the destruction of life arising from earthquakes, famine, volcanic eruptions and disease, which until comparatively recent times Iceland had little means of combating. In consequence there are many more women than men in Iceland. This primitive form of fishing persisted and as recently as 1922 nearly 1,000 rowing boats were still in operation.

One would never have suspected, when wandering about this little town, that it has the reputation of being one of the intellectual centres of Iceland, although it is in danger of losing this enviable character, as it becomes more commercialised. Many an old inhabitant is prepared to shake his head despondingly and say that the younger generation of Húsavíkians is more interested in objective forms of life than their fathers were. Certainly the younger generation are not prepared to look less up-to-date than the young men

State (Lutheran) Church
Akureyri

9. AKUREYRI
North Iceland

Second largest town in Iceland

10. above: *Old Farmhouses*; below: *typical Church*

and women of Reykjavík and Akureyri; which means, of course, that they vie with London and New York in appearance. It is admitted, however, that they tend to decorate their bodies more than their minds, and so the danger of the intellectual glory departing from Húsavík is very real.

My own experience favours the notion that these inhabitants of the far north are still interested in serious subjects, my public lectures being very well attended, the local priest, Sira Fridrik Fridriksson, a noted Lutheran minister and poetical critic and translator taking the Chair. It was computed that about one-tenth of the inhabitants of the town and district attended these three meetings, notwithstanding that many were at sea fishing and many busy haymaking while the weather was dry.

Winters in these northern regions can be bitterly cold, but the summers are correspondingly warm, and I found the weather delightful. The country in the vicinity is full of interest and some lovely farming land lies in the charming valley that runs on to Mývatn, undoubtedly the most beautiful lake in the country. On the whole this valley, or perhaps I ought to say, series of valleys, pleased me more than any other, which is saying a great deal. At Laugaskoli, a large farming centre about twenty-five miles from Húsavík and on the way to Mývatn, I lectured twice before groups of farmers who motored in from outlying districts. Here I met a famous Icelandic singer and his Italian wife who were on a summer vacation, and he assured me that his wife was delighted with the climate and scenery which, she said, closely resembled that of her native land—northern Italy.

This may seem incredible to those who think of Iceland after her name; but it is a fact that during my visit the weather was warm, the sun smiling down consistently from an Italian-like blue sky. It was so warm that visitors discarded their coats and walked about in their shirt sleeves.

Among the attractions of Húsavík is Laxá, a few miles south. Laxá is believed to be the finest salmon river in

Iceland and Iceland is virtually a salmon fishing country. This beautiful river flows swiftly out of Lake Mývatn to the sea, and at one point the visitor is invited to cross it by a sort of bucket, self-propelled over a wire rope. It was, however, out of order when I arrived.

There is, I fear, a danger of anyone who endeavours to describe many Icelandic beauty spots, passing from superlative to superlative with a monotony that is liable to spoil the very effect he may wish to create. Perhaps I ought to dismiss Lake Mývatn by merely advising the reader to see it for himself, as it certainly baffles the pen. Not only is it lovely, but it is also quaint, bizarre and horrific—a medley that only Nature is capable of doing justice to. I say without hesitation that Mývatn will live in my memory until my dying day. I wandered about it and its environs almost in a dream, trying to absorb and appreciate its beauty, magic and allure. Furthermore, it is situated in one of the loveliest of spots in one of Iceland's loveliest valleys. Its farms, too, are among the country's most prosperous. Indeed, an air of well-being and tranquility pervades all.

Mývatn is dotted with numerous small islands which on closer examination often turn out to be small volcanoes. Surrounding the lake are hundreds of similar volcanoes, and in about four hundred square yards I counted more than twenty of them! At some time or other the earth must have belched forth fire and fury, giving birth to the lake and its surroundings.

The shores of the lake contain immense deposits of lava taking on diabolical shapes, as only lava can. But tremendous and overpowering as all this is, one must walk to Dimmaborg, about two miles across country to realise how truly diabolical nature can be. I should have regarded Dimmaborg as the ultimate of grotesqueness had I not later travelled for more than an hour across the grim remains of the volcanic eruption of 1783, on my way to Kirkjuboejarklaustur, on the south coast. But more about that later.

Dimmaborg burst suddenly on the gaze of my two companions and me as we approached it from elevated ground.

It lies in a hollow caused, apparently, by a slight subsidence. The effect is both terrific and delightful; satisfying at the same time one's love of the beautiful combined with one's inquisitiveness of the grim and hideous. I sat down on the edge of the ruin and considered the strange scene before me, fascinated. It was the most extensive chamber of horrors I had ever seen. In imagination I watched Dante and Virgil walking through this veritable inferno, although today it can be as cold as ice notwithstanding that it was born of fire. It would require no small amount of nerve to pass through it at night time, especially if the moon were shining, because Dimmaborg is literally filled with strange figures, all sinister.

It is the abode of ogres and queer idols which, in the declining rays of the setting sun, appear to come to life and peer about. Dimmaborg is Icelandic for "Dark Castle," a fitting name since it seems to be filled with agonised souls pent up in deep dungeons. They are merged in the vast piles of black lava which stand out as a whole against the background of tall sinister-looking mountains. The impression grows on one that Nature thought the whole thing out, and forgot nothing that would add to this attractive monstrosity. Nature must literally have groaned with travail when giving birth to it.

But it, however, is not all darkness and horror. There are some delightful touches of charm off-setting its grimness, although some of them must be carefully looked for. Here and there pretty little silver birches and flowers grow among scanty patches of grass. It is fitting, also, that nestling in small crevices among the burnt-out lava are to be found some perfectly innocent-looking Lyfjagras—a carnivorous plant. Its method of snaring its victims is simple. Exuding a sticky substance, unseen by its intended victim which unsuspecting settles upon it and then finds it cannot escape; the vicious plant then slowly dissolves it and works it into the substance of its own being.

When at last my companions and I escaped from this Dark Castle, I looked back to take a farewell glance from the elevated rim which surrounds it, and watched two sturdy young Icelanders with travelling packs strapped to their shoulders descend into the abyss and disappear into the jaws of Gehenna. But they walked with bold and confident strides, as if familiar with the multitude of grotesque forms and faces which leered out upon them from almost every crevice in that black pile of dead earth.

The country immediately in the vicinity of Mývatn is thermal, a good deal of hot water flowing continuously into the lake. Deep down amid split lava rocks lay warm water in which swam men and women with evident enjoyment. The name Mývatn was given to the lake because at certain periods of the year it is infested with midges, none of which were present on this occasion. It is a paradise for those who fish for char and trout.

It has some curious local history, which like all local history in Iceland has become national. At Reykjahlid, or Steam Hill, stand two large guest houses, one very old, the other quite modern. Nearby is the doll-like church with its coloured roof, in the cemetery of which lie many of the local dead. The church is famous because of what is believed to be a special act of Providence on its behalf. The story is of more than passing interest because of the apparent evidence that stares the listener and critic in the face.

About thirty years ago, during a severe volcanic eruption which threatened to overwhelm and destroy the entire district, the flowing lava came stealthily down to Reykjahlid consuming everything in its path. Nothing seemed more certain of destruction than the church, the lava flowing directly towards it. Had the church been destroyed there was no hope for the nearby farms, and nothing short of a miracle could have averted the disaster. But in Iceland miracles do happen, as any Icelander will show you, and here was an example. From some inexplicable cause, the lava, when within a few yards of the church, suddenly ceased to flow and the neighbourhood was saved. There stands the lava, piled up close to the wall of the cemetery.

Mývatn will in time become one of the most popular

pleasure resorts in Iceland, owing to the removal of its present chief drawback—difficulty in reaching it, especially for those who live in the west, including Reykjavík. Plans are already being formed to build a large hotel there with modern equipment and accommodation. It is also hoped to build an airfield, linking Mývatn up with all the principal centres of the country.

The local Lutheran priest invited me and my party to tea at the vicarage and later showed us the church. This young clergyman was an excellent example of the farmer-priest, notwithstanding that at one time he had been Principal of a College. His farm was in every way one of the most up-to-date that I had seen, and he was evidently as interested in his flock of sheep as in his flock of parishioners.

The day previous to our arrival he had done what no other farmer in Iceland had attempted. The loss of sheep through straying in the mountains is considerable, and to find them parties of as many as forty or fifty people are employed—an expensive procedure. This young man had hit upon the idea of hiring a plane from Akureyri to fly over the mountains on the lookout for the lost sheep. During the flight he had passed over Askja, the largest volcanoe in the country, and Vatnajökull, the giant glacier. We could see both of these famous mountains—Vatnajökull is situated on a mountain—from his residence.

This clergyman spoke such perfect English that I mistook him for an Oxford graduate, but was surprised to learn that he had never left his native land.

CHAPTER 13

AKUREYRI ONWARD

AKUREYRI, the second largest town in Iceland, has a population of about 6,000 and its approach from Húsavík resembles in general most of the extensive journeys through the country. It was again a case of climbing stiff mountains and descending into steep valleys.

The first view of Akureyri is from the mountains on the opposite side of Eyjafjördur, on the west shore of which it lies. The situation is pretty, and as it has been built far down the fjörd it is safe from the violence of the northern sea. Because of this the climate is milder than would be expected from a city on the north coast and almost within sight of the arctic circle. Surrounded by lofty mountains which add much to the picturesqueness of the scene, they also shield it from winds. In summer Akureyri is on the whole brighter than Reykjavík, and often has much warmer weather, although on the average it is colder during all seasons of the year. It is unfinished, having few paved thoroughfares, and one can traverse it from end to end during a pleasant stroll.

Its excellent harbour ensures the constant presence of ships, and it is seldom without an airplane on the shore or a seaplane on the fjörd, there being a frequent service to Reykjavík and other parts of the island. Its principal architectural attraction is the unusually modern church which, situated on the steep side of the mountain at the foot of which much of the city nestles, towers majestically above the lower part of the town. To reach the church from the lower part it is necessary to climb eighty-eight steps. The interior is just as attractive as the exterior, and one is surprised to find so modern a building in this remote part of the world. During the military occupation, both American and British soldiers regularly filled the church at Sunday morning services.

I arrived 20th July on a sunny day and lectured twice in the Church Hall soon afterwards, the Reverend Fridrik Rafner, Vice-Bishop of Iceland, occupying the Chair. At dinner one evening he recounted to me an interesting story about a young sailor whom he, when a sailor before the mast, had known. This young sailor had an impressive dream, and being an Icelander attached significance to it, and informed the Bishop that he knew now that he would soon die by drowning. Shortly afterwards an accident happened to the ship which gravely endangered the life of the youngster, and the Bishop assured him that the event had "broken" the dream. But the young man sadly shook his head and said that he knew it was not so, and that he was doomed. His premonition proved to be correct. A day or so later he was accidently killed while landing from a rowing boat.

During my sojourn in Akureyri the Amateur Golf Championship was played and I caddied for one of the contestants. Every golfer of note in Iceland, including the Westmen Islands, took part, and an enthusiastic and earnest lot of sportsmen they were. The course, which was on a small plateau high up the mountain side, was about the worst imaginable; so bad, indeed, that no bunkers had been laid down. The greens without exception were like miniature mountain ranges, but the golfers found consolation in the fact that they all faced the same difficulties. The weather was fine but windy, and the general standard of play good, the winner going round in 84. The efficiency of these golfers spoke highly for their coaches, all of whom had been well-known British and American professionals.

While in Akureyri I visited the Co-operative Society's woollen mills and was impressed by the quality of the cloths manufactured and the efficient manner in which the undertaking was run. Some of the very latest machinery had been installed and some more was eagerly awaited from England. Returning to my hotel I was surprised at being hailed by a young fisherman standing with another member of the crew in a doorway. At first I failed to recognise him, but after I had penetrated behind his three days' growth of beard, I knew him to be one of Iceland's budding young artists, whose name is already known in the United States of America. He is a modernist in every way, influenced to some extent by the Picasso-Matisse School, and shows clearly the direction in which the younger school of Icelandic artists move.

He laughingly explained the reason for his unusual appearance. Having decided on a few weeks vactation he had signed on as a member of the crew of a fishing smack on a percentage basis dependent upon the catch. The prospects were, however, not good as after several days of fishing few fish had found their way into the nets. Even the fine spell of weather that he had encountered did not make up for this and for the inconvenience of the living quarters of the crew of nineteen.

There befell me while in Akureyri what is generally regarded as a most uncommon experience, for there are few thieves and pickpockets in Iceland, the criminal population is notably low.

I had gone to the post-office to send a telegram and experienced difficulty in making the young girl behind the counter understand me. When paying for the telegram I placed all my loose money on the counter inviting the clerk to take out of it what I owed, returning the remainder to my pocket. During this episode I had been several minutes in the post-office and had noticed a well-built woman of about sixty years of age, dressed in the national costume, leaning against the counter doing nothing, the young clerk paying no attention to her. She and I were the only occupants of the office, which was slack owing to it being Saturday afternoon. Nothing suspicious happened although my attention had been attracted by the curious way this Icelandic woman looked at me. It was not until I was well on my way back to the hotel that I discovered she had neatly picked my pocket of all it contained. I hurried back to the post-office, to find the woman still leaning nonchalantly against the counter, doubtless waiting for her next victim. It would have been useless to complain as I had no proof that she had robbed me, all Icelandic money being, of course, alike.

Nestling at the foot and on the lower slopes of mountain sides, Akureyri has little hope of becoming as big as Reykjavík and must devote its entire energies to commerce, although the surrounding hill sides are pitted with prosperous farms. Especially is this so of the hills across the bay, where some very old and famous farms still flourish.

It would be difficult to say which is the main street of Akureyri, but there can be no two opinions about the attractiveness of the roadway which runs along the edge of the bay and in which stands what I suppose must be called the Botanical Gardens with the tallest trees in Iceland. This and the park constitute the principal attractions of the town. I spent a whole morning in the park sitting in the sunshine among prettily-arranged flowers. All this gave to Akureyri a homeliness which I never felt in Reykjavík, because the park in the capital is not yet finished like that at Akureyri.

We left Akureyri for Saudárkrókur, on the west shore of Skagafjördur, on 24th July. Saudarkrókur is a typical Icelandic fishing village and has a population of about two hundred. Mr. Nikulas Fridriksson had undertaken to be both host and guide, kindly placing at my disposal his motor car.

Mr. Fridriksson, Inspector General of Reykjavík Municipal Electricity Works, was also a great patriot and thoroughly versed in the history of his country and I was very fortunate to have him plan this part of the itinerary. One of our objectives was to visit an old stone and turf church and Glaumbaer, an equally old turf and stone farm, recently acquired by the Government and preserved as a national memorial.

The church was situated on the bank of a small stream over which one could cross, either by stepping stones or a crude bridge constructed of three loosely bound boards, which threatened every moment to roll apart and deposit the intrepid passenger into the water below. It was certainly the most ancient building that I saw in Iceland, and was picturesque in its simple plainness. Small as most of the churches of this country are, this one had several genuine attractions, a brief study of which revealed that these old Icelanders knew well how to use their scanty materials to advantage.

The interior was very bare and unattractive, in common with all churches that I visited, with the exception of the beautiful modern structure at Akureyri, and in a less degree the cathedral in Reykjavík. One feature of this church was the somewhat commodious seats for the congregation. Most old Icelandic churches, and some modern ones too, have narrow high-backed seats, uncomfortable even to look at. The cause of this, I have been informed, was lack of material and, of course, lack of funds.

All this conformed strictly with the external appearance of the little building. The turf roof struck me as quite unable to keep out the rain, and I was surprised to find the interior definitely dry and at this time of the year comfortably warm. The turf walls had been carried about three feet beyond the wooden interior walls, for these were made of a sort of matchboarding. This gap gave ample air space and helped to keep the church dry and ventilated. The turf roof was well laid on a strong board ceiling and was quite weather proof.

Old as the church looked—it might well have been hundreds of years old, judged by the unpractised eye—it was little more than one hundred years old, and a standing testimony to the perishable nature of these old stone and turf edifices. In Iceland it is regarded as a very ancient building.

Glaumbaer is about the same age. From outside it is plain and unprepossessing as most other ancient Icelandic farms, but not less interesting because of that. It must not, I learned, be regarded as typical of the average farm of a century ago; but as a fair example of a particularly prosperous and well-to-do farm.

It consisted of several straggling buildings, all of which, upon closer inspection were placed in their positions by design, as all served a purpose both economical and useful. Thus, the barns and stalls were adjoining the house, enabling the inhabitants to obtain heat from the bodies of the animals; no small consideration a century ago when Iceland was without coal and depended upon whatever means she could find for heating purposes.

I was surprised at the dryness and thickness of the inside turf walls. In some places they must have been nearly two feet thick. With two exceptions the ground floors were of earth, beaten solid and dry by years of use. The guest room, easily the most comfortable and neatest in the house, was about ten feet square and panelled throughout.

The main living room was of turf and earth, without windows, unless the two small apertures set high at the ends of the gables be called windows. Glass was seldom used, the windows being covered with partially transparent fish skin, or the sac in which calves are born. In some old farms the living room, like the guest room, was made entirely of board.

In Glaumbaer the main living room afforded a clear idea of the discomforts to which the inhabitants were subjected when they lit a fire, the entire fireplace being constructed of brick standing well away from the wall, without a chimney, the smoke escaping as best it could through a hole in the roof. But what could let out the smoke could also let in the rain, and so one had to guess how the fire kept in in wet weather.

The interiors are naturally dim and at night time lighting was obtained about the time this farm was erected either from candles or oil lamps. In some instances lamps resembling those of the Ancient Romans were used, the wick floating in the oil. Glaumbaer amply demonstrated the discomforts old Icelanders must have experienced in their homes, especially in winter; and it is obvious why there was so much tuberculosis. It must be remembered that this model farm had most of the advantages which prevailed in Iceland in the middle of the 19th century. In smaller and poorer abodes, life must indeed have been hard.

Iceland never had any "good old days," and no reasonable Icelander can possibly desire a return to the past. It is doubtful whether Icelanders at the beginning of the 19th century were any better off than the serfs and villeins of the 13th and 14th centuries in England. It is surprising too that they did not make more use of stone when erecting their dwellings, as the island has plenty, both basalt and sandstone. One might be excused for concluding that owing to the lowness of these old farms, Icelanders were a short race; but Hooker writing about one hundred and forty years ago says that he saw some men at least six feet tall.

He also refers to the terrible state of the health of the people, sicknesses of a very grave nature prevailing, the common diseases being scurvy, leprosy, elephantiasis, jaundice, pleurisy, tuberculosis and *depression*. He attributed all to the misrule of the Danes; but it must be remembered that at the time he wrote Britain was at war with Denmark which espoused the cause of Napoleon, and part of his duty was to decry the enemy. It is obvious, however, that the Danes, who despised Icelanders, did little or nothing to alleviate their lot, and aimed at keeping the people ignorant; they certainly kept them poor. Hence the sad state of things prevailing in 1809, when the sick and lame were to be seen crawling about in every part of the island, pitiable objects of distress and misery.

At that time there was only one medical doctor in the whole of the country, and he resided in Reykjavík. Even as late as 1900 there was only one dentist in Iceland, and this was not because the people had superlative teeth.

Although lacking so much these humble people retained their interest in literature, practically all of them being able to read and write. This enabled them to keep their language pure. No doubt out of the habit of repeating the sagas grew their love of the marvellous. For pleasure they indulged in playing chess, wrestling, dancing and music, using crude home-made instruments, examples of which can be seen in the museum. Music was always a restricted pleasure, and declined along with dancing considerably during the worst periods of their national life. It is not, therefore, difficult to appreciate why Hooker so emphatically included depression among the prevalent diseases.

Another cause contributing to the purity of their language was the limited intercourse with the outside world. No strangers settled among them sufficiently long to make an impression on their mother tongue. The Anglo-American invasion may, from that point of view, prove a blessing, as it is obvious that when a language does not change over a long period it must be due to the absence of new ideas, espcially of modern science and mechanics. Icelandic scholars readily admit that the language is not sufficiently expressive of new ideas.

One would, on considering these various disadvantages, suppose that the morals of the people would have been gravely affected. Indiscriminately to sleep the sexes in the same room, for example, is not liable to encourage the highest moral conduct. Partly because of this habit there has long existed misleading stories about the sex relationships of Icelanders. Before leaving for Iceland in 1946 I conversed with soldiers who had been there during the occupation, and heard curious stories which I know now must have originated in the imagination of the recounters. There is, with perhaps one or two unimportant exceptions, no difference between the sex relationships of Icelanders and those of other civilised countries. The difference arises from the fact that an engagement may be regarded as equal to marriage; only some, not all, take advantage of this custom.

Few people were at one time more unjustly criticised than Icelanders, the climax of bitter invective and falsehood being reached by Anderson in his *History of Iceland*. His accusations did great harm and may not altogether have ceased to influence foreign opinion, although it must have been obvious to anyone that his remarks originated in the strongest prejudice. "The people," he writes, "know very little of God, or His will; for the value of sixpence, they will perjure themselves even to the prejudice of their nearest relations; full of wrath and revenge, extremely lascivious and vicious, and arrant thieves and cheats . . . continually indulging themselves in the filthy sin of drunkenness."

It is well-known, of course, that Icelanders have always been highly religious and many writers have commented, upon their sobriety.

Today Icelandic women are decidedly on the tall side, well-formed and handsome. The men are also well-made and athletic both in appearance and habits. Perhaps a greater sport-loving nation does not exist. The height of the present generation, especially the women, is generally attributed to their opulence since 1940. The effect of the war is obvious in another way: nowhere will you find so many young people in proportion to the population.

As for their character, since my arrival I have travelled extensively throughout the country under circumstances which enabled me to meet them in the privacy of their homes, both in town and country, and in large numbers at public meetings and private classes. There has not been a single incident to show that they do not rank among the most trustworthy people. Nor has there been any exaggeration in the oft repeated statement that they are by nature a highly cultured and artistic people.

Every house that I entered, even remotely situated farms, have had a good collection of books, often in several languages; and paintings are much in evidence. It is very striking to find oneself in a farm, perhaps miles from the nearest habitation, and see books written in Icelandic, English, Danish, Swedish and Norwegian; there is also often a good sprinkling of German works. Danish and English seem to be the most popular foreign languages; and an Englishman is never at a loss to find someone who can speak his language sufficiently well to hold a sustained conversation. There is everywhere the same passionate love of country. Probably no other race is more consistent in this respect.

They are a shy people, and their reserve is often mistaken for coldness and pride. I had some amusing conversations with British and American soldiers and sailors who mistook their reserve for antagonism, and in every case I found that the mistake arose partly from tales they had heard. In every instance, also, I found that these servicemen had, themselves, made no attempt to be friendly with Icelanders, expecting them to make the initial overtures.

My impression was that the basis of the servicemen's criticism was an inferiority complex, arising from a feeling that their uniform was no recommendation. No doubt this, in its turn, arose from being almost entirely conscripts; many of them being soldiers, sailors and airmen from compulsion and not from choice.

On one occasion a number of British sailors on a minesweeper gathered round me and freely expressed their complaints. All were impressed by the obvious prosperity of the Icelanders and this they seemed to resent. They complained that none of the inhabitants had spoken to them or appeared to notice them; but all admitted they, too, had not attempted to start a conversation. One sailor bewailed that Icelandic girls boycotted them, and his grounds for this accusation winnowed down to the fact that two young Icelandic girls had averted their heads when one of his friends tried to photograph them as they walked along the quay! It had not struck him that to attempt to do such a thing to strangers was ill-mannered. I suggested that they first break down their own reserve before passing judgment, and they admitted the logic of the advice.

The journey from Akureyri to Saudárkrókur took the car along the banks of charming rivers and through equally charming valleys, rich with cultivation, and capable of supporting a much larger population; especially the wide and luscious plains of Blonduhlid.

The more one explores the valleys and plains of east and north, the more one wonders how it is that they are so sparsely populated. It seems a pity that so much valuable land should lie idle while so many people in Europe are crying out for more space in which to live. The principal cause is, of course, the belief that Iceland has an uncongenial climate and is so mountainous as to be practically uninhabitable. Most people who have not travelled are unaware of the deceits of latitude, and because Iceland extends beyond the 66° they think it must be like a perpetual Christmas Day.

So misled are they that some writers have actually declared that reindeer are indispensable for practical purposes. True a few of them were introduced into the country from Norway in 1771, but they no longer prove useful and live in a wild state in the interior, although kept in reservations, but they are so few in number that they are seldom if ever seen. With all my searching I found not one. Before 1900 they were practically exterminated, but have been protected during the last three or four decades. Nor do polar bears live here, although they are sometimes carried to Iceland from Greenland on ice-floes, but they are always immediately destroyed.

There are very few wild animals on the island, and none of them of great economic importance. Wild foxes, which were formerly quite common, were virtually exterminated because of the serious damage they did on the farms. Now they are almost entirely bred in captivity for their pelts; and silver, platinum, and blue and white foxes' skins are a considerable source of income.

While on the subject of Icelandic pelts, which have always been popular throughout the world, mink and sheep skins constitute the only others that are exported. Mink and fox skins go as far afield as New Zealand.

The pasture lands of Blönduhlíd extend, as one approaches to Saudárkrókur, to Saemundarhlíd, and present a pleasing picture. The river here breaks into a number of wide channels, which converge and separate again, until they pour their waters into Skagafjördur, one of the widest fjörds. Long before this, however, Drangey comes into view, a tall, rocky island, half way up the fjörd, and noted for having been the final abode and death place of Grettir Asmundsson, a famous outlaw.

Grettir's fame has been greatly enhanced by his having swum from his island home to procure fire for his lair. This deed necessitated his running the gauntlet of his enemies, as well as keeping the burning peat alight while he returned; but this he did in a boat.

He succeeded in returning to Drangey although his identity was discovered notwithstanding his disguise. He was eventually killed in 1030, through the carelessness of one of his fellow bandits.

From Saudárkróker we motored to Hólar to see the burial place of Bishop Jón Arason and his two sons.

It may seem strange that these three men should have become heroes in a country so firmly Protestant. There is only one Roman Catholic Church, an imposing edifice, standing high in the west end of Reykjavík, and has, it is said, less than one hundred worshippers.

The deaths of Bishop Jón Arason and his two sons are connected with the Protestant Reformation and the introduction of Lutheranism into Iceland during the first half of the sixteenth century. Jón Arason was head of the Roman Catholic Church in Iceland and refused to yield to the new faith, introduced by Christian III and adopted by the Althing as the national faith. He showed fight and paid for his temerity with his head and those of his sons. There was a good deal that was illogical about this intrepid man. He denounced, for instance, a bishop because he had a wife, while he took to himself a concubine by whom he had five sons and two daughters.

Because he refused to renounce his faith and adopt the new one Jón Arason was proclaimed an outlaw by the King of Denmark. But Jón had previously appealed to the Pope for support and received a letter from him urging him not to betray the Church of Rome. The Bishop lost no time in calling together the clergy and laymen to whom, in the Church at Hólar, he read the Papal letter. He then gathered a force of four hundred armed men and marched to Thingvellir where he defied the Althing, overawed them, and deposed the Speaker, installing his illegitimate son Ari in his place.

From there he proceeded to Skálholt, a few miles away,

and finding the garrison prepared to fight, he placed a Protestant Bishop whom he had captured in front of his men as a mark for their missiles and compelled them to surrender. After that he consecrated the little church at Skálholt which, he declared, had been defiled by the new faith; dug up the corpse of Bishop Gizur who had died a short time previously, and had it interred outside the churchyard in unconsecrated ground, as the corpse of a heretic. Proclaiming himself lawful administrator of the diocese, he concluded proceedings by consecrating a priest in the church, after the approved Roman fashion. He then made a round of the western coast, visiting monasteries and reconsecrating churches, returning eventually to Hólar confident that he had succeeded in getting all backsliders to return to the old faith, with one exception. His two priestly sons approved of his drastic proceedings, and as a consequence shared his fall and his untimely fate.

There, however, remained one man, Dadi Gudmundsson whom he realised he must subdue before he could feel perfectly secure, and with a number of armed followers he marched against him, only to meet a stronger force and utter defeat. He was arrested, tried and condemned to an indefinite sentence. His enemies, however, determined to destroy him.

On Friday, 7th November, 1550, a simple block was erected in the courtyard of what is euphemistically called by one writer "a palace" at Skálholt, and he and his sons were decapitated. The scene of the execution is today marked by a simple stone monument, there being, as far as I could see, no indication that there had been a building there. After lying exposed for some hours the three bodies were buried in the churchyard behind the choir.

A few months later thirty men, accompanied by three priests, unexpectedly arrived at Skálholt and receiving permission from the officiating Bishop, removed the bodies and carried them to Hólar, where they were buried with much ceremony. Today their bodies lie just outside the church door, and whoever enters the church must necessarily walk over them. They were looked upon as saints, and at the time of their reburial many miracles of healing are said to have been wrought on the sick who succeeded in touching the casket in which lay the body of the Bishop.

Time has not dimmed Jón Arason's fame. Today there exists a public subscription for erecting a suitable memorial to his memory. His adherents and relations were, on the whole, treated with clemency; but most of the valuables belonging to the cathedral were, by orders of the Danish king, taken to Copenhagen and never returned. This is still a source of resentment in Iceland.

When I visited the church there was little of an outstanding nature to speak of its former grandeur. It is the oldest building in Iceland, having been erected about 450 years ago. Jón Arason was undoubtedly a powerful, if intolerant man, fond of pomp, but withal kindly. He lives still as a poet of renown, and families in Iceland count it a great distinction to be his descendants. He may be regarded as the last bastion of the Church of Rome in Iceland to fall before the triumphant march of Lutheranism.

On the way to Hólar we passed along the best highway in Iceland, and it showed what can be accomplished. It was built up to an average height of about three feet most of the way to keep it dry as it passes over an extensive marshland. It crossed this bog for at least two miles, the foundations standing firm, and the surface excellent.

One can best appreciate the significance of such roads when it is remembered that up to the end of last century all transport in the interior of Iceland was done by pack-ponies; carts were almost unknown even fifty years ago and the so-called roads were mere cart tracks. Sixty years ago even the street of Reykjavík were blocked to traffic apart from ponies by boulders of lava.

It was not until 1884 that any serious attempt was made to develop proper highways and the authorities were so ignorant of how to proceed that they had to engage the services of an expert from Norway to teach them. Ten years after it was enacted by law that cart roads should, at the expense of the State, be built from the chief towns into the country. Even as recent as 1925 many of the mountain roads which today are among the best highways of the country, were only bridle paths.

The question of bridges has always been a pressing one and has not yet been completely solved. Iceland is simply honeycombed with rivers and streams, many of them being ever changing glacier rivers. The foundations of these are so unstable that to span them would involve tremendous expense owing to the necessity of extending the bridges across very wide expanses to make them secure. Today there are more than three hundred over ten metres in length!

Hólar is situated at the end of a mountainous valley and so cut off from the surrounding country that it seems strange than Jón Arason should have chosen such a spot for his sanctuary. To reach it members of his flock had to take long and arduous journeys, sometimes along tortuous mountain paths. It seems unlikely that many people could have found time to travel to the church. A peculiar feature of the landscape the day I was at Hólar was the lowness of the clouds which descended right into the valley; but this phenomenon is not uncommon in Iceland.

The country between Saudárkrókur and Hólar is noted for its fine breed of ponies, the finest in the country, and it is said to be the aspiration of all pony lovers to possess one of them. We passed several of these hardy little creatures and they certainly lived up to their reputation. They are not only famous for their strength, speed and endurance, but also for their handsome appearance, fine glossy coats and long flowing manes.

CHAPTER 14

REYKHOLT AND SNORRI STURLUSON

ON the way to Reykholt we passed a number of small turf and stone farms, giving a good idea of how almost the entire country looked a hundred years ago. The impression was not altogether agreeable as they bore the impress of poverty; but this impression may have been misleading, as, in all probability, those old farmers were comfortably off. Lack of material rather than lacks of means, may have been the determining factor. In any case, it was obvious that in this particular district farmers had not thought it worth while to scrap their old homes in favour of modern concrete farms.

Sheep pounds seem to be built in the same manner all over the island, and they also make no pleasing impression, being invariably constructed of crude blocks of lava piled one above the other, the colour of them being a disagreeable dark brown, grey or black. They were by no means neat. Nevertheless, the erection of these walls require considerable patience and skill. At this time of the year none of them contained sheep, as they were left to run wild on the plains and mountains.

Icelandic sheep are a special feature and are to be seen almost everywhere in the open country. I saw none wandering about the villages as one so often sees in the villages of South Wales. They enjoy freedom from spring to autumn, and are rounded up as soon as the cold weather sets in. They are bold and pleasing creatures, with a surprising number of black, brown and piebald among them. Lambing starts later than in Britain, and it appears to be common for ewes to give birth to two and even more lambs; mother and offspring are to be seen grazing contentedly side by side, or exploring mountain sides, and often leaping sure-footedly across the crevices of lava fields. So sure-footed are they that no green spot on the steep mountain sides escape their attention.

The cows are almost as bold as the sheep and goats, and even these large animals may be seen grazing high up the mountains, in what look like inaccessible places. Iceland's cows and bulls are smaller than our own, but there are plenty of them. Goats are not so plentiful, and they so closely resemble sheep that they can be mistaken for each other from the distance. Flocks and herds are cultivated for home consumption, there being very little meat exported.

Here and there hamlets will be seen nestling usually on the shore of a fjörd. It is difficult to realise that large fortunes have been made out of these isolated settlements, and that not a few of Iceland's wealthiest citizens have been born and lived their lives in them. It is always noticeable how close together farms and their outhouses are, the reason being, of course, to save walking in severe wintry weather as well as to gain what heat may be thus obtained.

As we sped along an ever-changing scene met our gaze. When nearing Baula, a magnificent sharp-peaked mountain, we met with an irritating delay arising from the narrowness of the highway. We were travelling along, slightly above the level of the valley, when a private car, coming from the opposite direction, pulled up and the driver requested us to draw into a siding as a large lorry was approaching, too wide to permit us to pass. The car then hurried on to the next automobile with the same request, and soon every car travelling south on the long stretch of highway was parked by the side of the road.

No one seemed disturbed by this interference, evidently regarding it as inevitable and for the good of the community notwithstanding that half an hour elapsed before the lorry hove in sight carrying a huge road-levelling machine that had broken down and was on its way to be repaired. My companions had made themselves comfortable on the hillside, chatting and idly throwing stones into a pretty mountain cataract.

The narrowness of the highways can often be a trouble, as we experienced on more than one occasion. Once at least the inconvenience was not without an element of danger as we met a road-repairing machine blocking our path, and we had to reverse for about a quarter of a mile on an elevated roadway. A slight mistake would have sent us over the edge on to the field below.

There are, however, very few motor car accidents in Iceland owing to the skill of the drivers. Strangely enough the most dangerous strips of highway are the macadamised ones running out of Reykjavík. These encourage the more reckless drivers to increase their speed and accidents are therefore more frequent. Motoring in Iceland is about as safe as anywhere in the world, judging from my experience. During my stay I witnessed only one accident, and that was a slight one in Reykjavík. The fastest cars are invariably the long-distance 'buses, which are often over-crowded.

One serious 'bus accident did happen while I was there and Mr. Fridriksson motored me to the spot where it occurred. It was on one of those truly dangerous bends determined more by the nature of the terrain than by the folly of man. Mountains are cumbersome things, and one is often compelled to yield to their dictates where road-making is concerned. The spot where this accident happened was an abrupt descent and sharp bend on to the edge of a deep and dangerous gorge. At this point the car's brakes had failed, and the driver had the presence of mind to steer for a small plateau on the edge of the precipice, hoping that the 'bus would turn over before plunging to destruction in the gorge, where death was certain, either by the force of the impact or by drowning. Fortunately it turned over, but caught fire, many passengers being injured but none killed. I saw the remains of the 'bus—a mass of twisted metal and charred wood.

Soon after this we alighted to see the famous Glanni Falls, noted for its salmon. To reach it we walked across an excruciating deposit of lava with a wonderful mountain setting. To the north stood a mountain that looked like a mass of grey ashes, every particle of life having been burned out of it. Everywhere was evidence of some mighty prehistoric volcanic eruption.

On reaching these pretty falls, small in size compared with many other famous falls, we saw large numbers of salmon trying to leap up them; apparently with little success. Glanni Falls have two cascades, one somewhat larger than the other. The larger cascade is less fierce than the smaller, and one would have thought the salmon would have chosen to ascend this, but they chose the other. Their persistence was amazing. One big fellow, after several fruitless endeavours, came to grief by striking the ragged side of the cascade and may have been killed, for he appeared no more. Nature must have endowed these creatures with a terribly strong instinct to cause them to endanger their very existence through it.

The highway from Glannis Falls to Reykholt, like all other Icelandic highways, constantly opened new vistas of beauty and magnificence at every mile. Particularly attractive were Langjökull, the second largest glacier in Iceland with Thorisjökull standing close against it, and a few miles away, Ok, one of the smallest glaciers on the island. The countryside was rich with grass and extremely prosperous-looking. The valleys about here lie well inland and are profusely fertile, being supplied with ample water from the glaciers; while the valley in which stands Reykholt, where Snorri Sturlusson, the great saga writer and historian lived, is largely thermal.

It is fitting that the home of Iceland's greatest historian should be a centre of education. If his shade ever visits the place where he wrote so well, it must be delighted at the care taken by the authorities of the youngsters who, during the summer vacation, spend the nightless days of June, July and August at Reykholt. We met several parties of these children on which the future of Iceland so much depends, marching along happily under the care of teachers. It would have been impossible to have found a healthier and more contented body of youngsters.

At Reykholt, too, I saw something of their hardiness, for while standing near Snorri's bath, a party of about twenty children, ranging between the ages of four and eight years, came rushing out of the school-building, shouting with glee, clothed in nothing but shorts. A cold wind was blowing at the time, such as would have caused the mothers of England to dress their children in woollens; but these descendants of the old Vikings were of sturdier stuff, and evidently thought the weather ideal. Nearby a party of young girls reclined on the grass reading and chatting, paying no heed to the stranger from overseas. Icelanders are charmingly casual, and although about the most pure-blooded nation in the world, make it a habit of treating strangers as if they were fellow citizens.

Snorri Sturluson, born A.D. 1178, is regarded as one of the greatest personalities Iceland has produced. A man of considerable learning and great persistence, he was in many respects unusual. We are indebted to him for *The Heimskringla*, a saga which gives a graphic account of the history of the kings of Denmark, Norway and Sweden. One has only to see Reykholt to realise how wisely he selected the place of his abode; it was here also that his life was cut short in 1241, at the age of sixty-three, by an assassin. As I stood by the fine modern school erected on the ground where Snorri had built his principal farm and homestead, and looked down the lovely Reykholtsdalur valley, I could not avoid a feeling of admiration for his fine sense of the beautiful and the good. The valley contains several hot springs, most of which he utilised, for Snorri owned several farms.

The various accounts of his life leave a good deal of doubt on minor points, although the main features are clear. He was, in addition to being a great historian, no mean politician. By all accounts he was unscrupulous and prepared to gain his ends by any means in his power. It is recorded, as an example of this, that when he had a legal matter in dispute before the Althing, he enforced his claims with armed men numbering on occasions between six and eight hundred. This argument for the legality of a claim was by no means restricted to Snorri Sturluson, however, but was often adopted, in the early days of the settlement, by others. It is agreed that intellectually Snorri was head and shoulders above his contemporaries, who both feared and respected him. In addition, he was very rich.

Love of wealth spoiled his character, and eventually caused his death. Being of royal descent, he had much to support his influence and stimulate his pride, for Snorri was undoubtedly a snob. Throughout life he held the influential position of godi, and this office gave him legal and political power. At one time this position carried with it priestly functions and rights.

He lived at a time when it is believed the standard of living in Iceland was on a par with that of Denmark and England; which meant that the poor were very poor and the rich very rich. That Snorri appreciated comfort is amply demonstrated by the open-air warm water bath, supplied from a natural spring, which stands within a few yards of the spot where his residence had formerly stood. In shape it is similar to a Roman bath, being about four yards square and well-lined with cut freestone, the water being conducted by a covered drain or pipe. He did not, as is commonly believed, construct this bath himself, as there is evidence that it existed in the tenth century and must, therefore, have been made by one of the earliest settlers. Snorri renovated it, and used it in a manner not to be improved upon today. One of his additions was an underground tunnel leading from his house, which was discovered recently; and although this tunnel has become narrowed by the weight of the earth, it is still sufficiently high and wide to permit a man to pass through it. It must have required no small amount of labour to construct it, as it is cut through solid rock, crude blocks of which line the sides with edges sharp enough to demand care when passing through it. Doubtless the presence of hot water was one of the reasons why Snorri chose to live in this valley, as not only are there ample supplies of hot and cold water, but also good salmon fishing no great distance off. The steam of several hot springs is to be seen issuing from various parts of the valley.

Snorri appears to have been an exceedingly quarrelsome

man, falling out even with his own children. He contracted a second marriage during the lifetime of his first wife, whom he divorced. Samuel Laing accuses him of having embittered his family against himself to such an extent that his three sons-in-law murdered him; but later writers accuse his two step-sons of this crime. The story of his life is said to have been composed by one of his kinsmen, with whom he had been on bad terms; but even if allowance be made for the bias that would taint such an account, he appears to have been "greedy, selfish, ambitious; determined to gratify his avarice and evil passions." This strong language has since been modified by other biographers, who maintain that he was by no means as bloodthirsty as most of the chieftains of his day, but it is always admitted that he was avaricious, ambitious and perfidious.

Although it was not until his forty-third year that he made his first visit to Norway to gather information about the history of the kings of that country, as well as Denmark and Sweden, he is believed to have worked for some time previously on the subject, and by this first and subsequent visits confirmed the correctness of the information he had gathered in Iceland. While in Norway he moved in royal circles and was able to obtain information that could not have been recorded otherwise. His style is good although lacking in sentiment and feeling, which, however, in no way weakens the reliability of his work. Like all other Icelandic sagas something is lost in translation, even when his technical excellence is maintained.

The worst charge made against Snorri is that he visited Norway to betray the independence of his country, thus helping to subject it to Norway; but today no one seems to take this charge seriously. That his tastes were such as would make him appreciate the relative splendours of the Norwegian Court of the thirteenth century is evident, as he was naturally extravagant, evidence of which is found in the fact that his residence was magnificent for those primitive times. In Norway he became cup-bearer to King Hakon, a position equal to that of Chamberlain, or perhaps identical with it. This doubtless to some extent accounts for the suspicions of those who believed him to be a traitor; and it certainly fits in with his extremely materialistic love of life.

His materialism is shown in his saga which tends to become tedious because of monotonous descriptions of bloodshed, and the imagery of war. Nevertheless, it is full of valuable information of the highest historic value, throwing considerable light on the beliefs and practices of the times recorded.

Snorri was also a good poet and took considerable pride in it, having sought international fame. His desire appears to have been to gain honour as an outstanding poet, and it was that as much as anything that led him to Norway. Poets are still held in high estimation by Icelanders, and in the thirteenth century this ideal was as strong as it is today. As a politician Snorri ranked sufficiently high to be chosen as Speaker of the Althing or parliament.

The story of his death is pathetic. When members of his family determined to put up with his violence and greed no longer, they took an edict passed by King Hakon, which condemned him to death as a traitor, and attacked him in his house at Reykholt. Realising his danger, Snorri fled to the cellar where he was found, and where his assassins coolly killed him. The name of his murderer and of the man who gave the order for his death-blow to be struck have been preserved; "Gissur's servant, Simon Knut, bade the man, Arne Beisk, by name, to kill Snorri." On Simon Knut ordering the blow to be struck, Snorri, relying on his authoritative power said, "Thou shalt not strike," but the man gave the blow which despatched a truly great if faulty personality.

CHAPTER 15

HVÍTÁ AND BORG

ON the 26th July I was initiated into the art and mystery of salmon fishing in the river Hvítá. My instructor, Mr. Nikulas Fridriksson, was an enthusiast and an expert. Salmon fishing is under strict supervision in Iceland, inspectors having been put in control over their particular reaches.

The inspector to whom we applied was a substantial farmer, residing about a mile from the Hvítá, and like other Icelanders, insisted on treating us like friends and not mere clients. He invited us into his house and made us share an excellent tea with his family. This entailed a long gossip between our host and my Icelandic friends, who might have known the farmer all their lives, judging by the easy manner in which they behaved.

Not understanding Icelandic I was left more or less to my own devices, except every now and then when, out of courtesy the party spoke English, giving me at least an inkling of their conversation. They were all deeply interested in the Government's new hydro-electric scheme, intended, by the following autumn, to supply every farm in that district with electric light and power. One hundred farms would benefit, and it would all be accomplished by harnessing some waterfall. This fine example of the forward policy of the rulers of the country had won the enthusiastic endorsement of all the farmers.

The farmer was a hardy-looking man with perfect manners, and from his library showed that his interests exceeded the growing of crops and raising of sheep and cattle. I noticed he was wearing a pair of peculiar shoes made of sheep skin. They were, I found, a type used in Iceland long before foreign shoes were imported. They fitted the feet almost like gloves, the soles being no thicker than the uppers, the colour resembling mildew. The manner in which they were prepared is simple, and done entirely by the farmers themselves. I never saw them worn in towns.

The hair was first removed from the skin, which was then stretched on a wall to dry, after which it was cut to the shape of the feet and sewn. They were then well-soaked in water and placed on the feet while still wet to enable them to contract to the size and shape of the feet, and left to harden. It is surprising that although these shoes looked none too durable they were worn all day: in the house as slippers and in the fields inside rubber boots. Occasionally these sheep skin footwear were made up as boots, and then generally worn by townsfolk. That was probably why I failed to notice them when in the various cities.

No Icelandic home that I was privileged to enter was luxuriously furnished, but all were attractive and often made beautiful by flowers. This farmhouse was a case in point. I saw no flowers growing out of doors, but the house was well supplied, especially with ferns, for which Icelanders show a great liking. Perhaps the climate and the soil make it difficult to grow flowers out of doors; but inside the additional warmth produced a profusion of plants. It is strange that so few flowers grace the farms, while the towns, especially Reykjavík, have plenty.

By comparison the Icelandic farm labourers fare much better than the British. I observed no great difference between master and man, and, indeed, can recall no instance in which, without a previous intimation, I was able to distinguish the farmer from his employees. They often share the farmhouse with the farmer and his family; in the old days this was almost an invariable rule. The farmhouse, in this case—and it was typical of the district—had water laid on. Electric light and sanitation were all that could be desired, and this, notwithstanding the fact that, from the British standpoint, the farm was an isolated one.

If the following description of English farms and farm workers be true, and doubtless it is, then I saw in the whole of this island nothing so bad, but much that was infinitely better. To quote from one author writing about conditions of the English farm labourers: "Hard is the lot of the farm worker's wife living in a cottage perhaps three miles from a shop, where water is fetched from a pump outside, where sanitation may mean a hovel at the bottom of the garden, where all cooking and heating must be done by coal or wood fire, and where there is a 'bus perhaps but twice daily." This writer insists that the interiors of these wretched homes were grim, grimy, dingy and dirty, worse even than the filthy slum hovels that disgrace so many of our cities. It is astonishing how superior in many respects this little country, Iceland, is to some of the so-called great ones, both in standard of living and education.

Icelanders have an uncanny weather sense, and I was never once misled by them. This particular farmer foretold rain on the morrow, and on passing through his farm at 8.30 p.m., the farm hands were hurriedly working in the hay-fields in view of this prospect. The following day it was extremely wet and windy. It was here, too, that for the first time I noticed the remarkable effect of the sun upon distant mountains, while we were among storm clouds. It was very fine, the mountains showing with remarkable distinctness in a galaxy of golden light, with brown and green predominating. We were not successful in our piscatorial efforts, and after a few experiments I came to the conclusion that salmon fishing required great skill and patience.

Our failure however, was not reflected in the various guest houses at which we dined, especially in the region of Borganes, fresh water fish being served at every meal, salmon and trout especially. In country districts hereabouts salmon is often so common that even dogs refuse to eat it, and farm employees when signing a contract insist on the insertion of a clause in the Agreement to the effect that they will not be served salmon at meals more than twice a week. Farmers near Hvítá depend so upon salmon for their livelihood, that when one of them was accosted with "What a beautiful country this is! " replied, "It is when the salmon fishing is good."

The road from Hvítá to Borganes passes through the most extensive arable land of the whole island, stretching from the western coast to the southern and eastern shores of Hunafjördur, and is rich in history. Borganes is a small busy town, a port and a centre of fishing. The chief interest in this area lies a few kilometres westward, where stands Borg, an historical church.

We had the good fortune to be entertained by the handsome young officiating priest, whom I had met some time previously in Reykjavík. It is unnecessary to state that he took us into his house and treated us with the liberal courtesy that I had by now come to regard as one of the most reliable features of these charming people.

The chief difference between the Icelandic clergyman and others that I have met, is their total lack of an air of superiority. Yet they must be among the best informed and certainly among the broadest-minded and tolerant of Christian ministers.

The principal feature of Borg is the grave of Kjartan, perhaps Iceland's greatest hero. I am glad to say that no stone marks the last resting place of this remarkable man, who died all too young; instead, it is defined by an extensive, oblong, grass-covered mound, evidently meant to convey the fact that he was taller and physically larger than his fellows.

More than nine hundred and fifty years have passed since he met his untimely fate at the hand of his foster-brother, who will go down to history as one who took advantage of the kindness of the man who loved him too well.

The story of Kjartan is one of the epics of the earlier settlers in Iceland, and reveals how truculent they were, and what strange notions of courage and chivalry they sometimes entertained. The saga which tells the facts is unlit by a single philosophical thought, although it has much to say about courage, boldness, hatred, vindictiveness and treachery, in which woman comes out no better than man. It makes one wonder how anyone survived in those savage times, when the founders of Iceland gave birth to a bloody brood. It seems strange that from such desperate men of war a nation of farmers and fishermen should have developed, noted for their peacefulness.

The sagas show that the old Norseman was a proud and snobbish person, more concerned with what he regarded as the honour of himself and his family than with justice. Yet today in Iceland all men are equal in a realistic sense to be found nowhere else. The first consideration of these early settlers seems to have been whether this man or woman was socially fit to become a member of the family. To marry out of one's social caste was to dishonour the family, unless some special compensation could be counted upon. They were not averse to having paramours, and out of such an alliance came Kjartan, the bravest, strongest, most handsome and honourable of them all.

The beginning of the story goes back to just before the middle of the tenth century when Hoskuld, the grandfather of Kjartan, went to Norway and bought a beautiful Irish slave. This woman was believed to be deaf and dumb, but she was so attractive that her owner demanded twice as much for her than for any other of his slaves. Having made his purchase Hoskuld returned to Iceland A.D. 948, and shortly afterwards the woman gave birth to a male child, whom Hoskuld named Ólaf. Ólaf, as a child, was extremely pretty and grew to be a handsome man. Because of the great care with which he dressed and the splendid manner in which he kept his weapons, he was nicknamed "The Peacock."

When Ólaf was about two years old Hoskuld, who had never heard the boy's mother speak, was amazed to hear her talking to the child, and on demanding why she had pretended to be dumb, was informed by her that it was because of the peculiar circumstances of her life. She was, she revealed, the daughter of an Irish king who had been captured, at the age of fifteen, by Vikings. By pretending to be dumb she thought it might add to her chances of escaping slavery. Thereafter Hoskuld treated both her and the child with great consideration, and in course of time Ólaf married Thorgerd, the daughter of Egil, a neighbouring chieftain.

Thorgerd at first objected to the marriage on the grounds that Ólaf was the son of a slave, but was finally persuaded to accept him because his mother, being a princess, was really more highly-born than Ólaf's father, who also came of a noble family. From this marriage Kjartan was born A.D. 978.

Kjartan grew to be even more handsome than his father and became a wonderful athlete, with a disposition as fine as his body. Through his pleasant temperament he won the deepest affection from his fellows, who from the first, were willing to follow him wherever he went. When about twenty years of age he fell in love with Gudrun, a young widow, the daughter of a chieftain, and she reciprocated his affection. Gudrun was a woman of strong mind, and as subsequent history proved, vindictive and treacherous. Throughout the saga she appears as an evil genius responsible for rancour and bloodshed. In the end, after her wickedness had caused the deaths of several splendid men, and the banishment of five of her own brothers, she repented and turned religious.

Gudrun was anxious to marry Kjartan and settle down, but he had made up his mind to go to Norway, and when he informed her she objected. Kjartan, however, refused to turn from his project, and tried in vain to extract a promise from Gudrun that she would wait for him three years, and if he did not return by that time to consider herself free to marry someone else. Kjartan was accompanied to Norway by Bolli, his foster-brother, who was almost Kjartan's equal in age, appearance, strength and prowess. All through his life Kjartan showed great affection for Bolli who appeared to return it in full measure; but in the end jealousy caused him mercilessly to kill Kjartan.

On their arrival at Norway Kjartan and his companion

were well-received and learned that the old King had died and that his son, Ólaf Tryggvason, had ascended the throne. Ólaf was unknown to Kjartan and they met each other in a strange way. One day from their vessel Kjartan and Bolli saw a young Norwegian giving a remarkably fine exhibition of swimming. Kjartan, concluding that he was merely showing off, suggested that Bolli, who was also a fine swimmer, should dive in and show the stranger who was the better man; but Bolli refused on the grounds that Kjartan was a better swimmer than he, and should teach the upstart the lesson, whereupon Kjartan dived into the sea and approached the stranger. The result was some remarkable horseplay on the part of Kjartan and the young Norwegian, in which they seem to have come off equally well. Eventually the stranger revealed his identity—he was none other than Ólaf Tryggvason, the King.

Ólaf Tryggvason was destined to play an important part in the history of Iceland, at that time under Norwegian rule. Ólaf had embraced Christianity and determined that Iceland should follow suit. So enthusiastic was he for the new faith that he was prepared to stop at nothing to propagate it, and threatened to destroy any of his subjects who rejected Christianity. Himself a powerful preacher, Ólaf Tryggvason combined the profession of priest with that of kingship, and preached in church.

From the moment that he met Kjartan, Ólaf developed a strong affection for him and tried to convert him to his new religion. Ólaf made no secret of his reasons for virtually courting the favour of his popular subject: Kjartan's influence, he said, was so great among his fellow countrymen that if he embraced Christianity, the complete conversion of Iceland would be assured. Kjartan, however, indignantly rejected the royal proposal and threatened to kill the King if he persisted. The King hearing of this through his spies sent for Kjartan and informed him that he was aware of what he had said; but instead of executing him, which would have been in strict accord with the policy of the time, he forgave him and left him at liberty.

This clemency so impressed Kjartan and his friends that they agreed to become Christians and were publicly baptised, although Kjartan rejected the King's suggestion that he return to Iceland to convert, by force if necessary, his fellow-countrymen. He remained, at the express wish of the king, at court, where he and Bolli were greatly respected. It is evident that Kjartan understood the temper of his fellow-countrymen on the subject of religion, as that summer Hjalti Skeggjason was outlawed by the Althing for blaspheming the gods.

The king decided to send emissaries to Iceland for the purpose of compelling the people to accept Christianity, and Bolli accompanied the expedition. It is evident that Bolli was at the time under the impression that Kjartan had abandoned the idea of marrying Gudrun owing to the attention he had been paying Ingibjorg, the King's sister, who was known to be in love with him; he even broached the subject to Kjartan, who declared, however, that he was not seriously interested in the princess.

Arriving in Iceland A.D. 1000, Bolli lost no time in making love to Gudrun himself, Gudrun enquired whether anything more than the King's affection for Kjartan kept him in Norway, and Bolli informed her of the rumours respecting his attachment to the king's sister. Although this news upset Gudrun she rejected Bolli's proposal, assuring him that she could never think of marrying anyone while Kjartan was alive; Bolli replied that in that case he feared that she would remain a widow a long time. Later on Bolli renewed his suit and Gudrun finally agreed to marry him. The following year Kjartan returned home, and on hearing of Gudrun's marriage seemed to be in no way displeased. Gudrun on the other hand was terribly upset, and showed it so plainly that people openly said that she was pining for Kjartan.

Later Kjartan began to pine for her and became unfriendly towards Bolli. The family, realising the serious consequences that might follow a feud between these two persuaded Kjartan not to grudge Bolli his happiness, but himself to marry. Their choice fell upon a beautiful girl named Hrefna; Kjartan consented and after the marriage lived happily with his bride.

It appears, however, that deep in the minds of Gudrun, Bolli and Kjartan bitterness remained and soon bubbled up with dire results. Gudrun was never reconciled to Kjartan's marriage, while Kjartan at the first opportunity insulted Gudrun, whose dislike for his wife he resented. A few months after Kjartan's marriage he arranged a big feast at his home, Herdholt, to which Gudrun and her husband were invited, and Kjartan, on two occasions, seized the opportunity of deliberately offending Gudrun, with a view to showing her that he regarded Hrefna as her superior. Gudrun retaliated by stealing Kjartan's much prized sword which had been presented to him by the King. He held this weapon in superstitious regard, the King having assured him that so long as he used it his life would be safe. To Gudrun must also be attributed the mysterious disappearance of Hrefna's coif, which had been presented to Kjartan by Princess Ingibjorg on his leaving Norway.

The princess, thinking Kjartan would marry Gudrun, had given him the coif as a wedding present to Gudrun, but Kjartan gave it to Hrefna. It was very beautiful and Gudrun much resented the head-dress being given to her successful rival, whom she openly declared to be unworthy of it. Gudrun's object now was to make Bolli and Kjartan seriously quarrel, and she seized this opportunity to fan their smouldering resentment into a flame. Kjartan had, shortly before, angered Bolli by objecting to a land purchase he had made, doing his utmost to make the original owner cancel the contract by speaking more or less disparagingly of his foster brother. The sword was recovered, Kjartan's men finding it hidden in a ditch, but the scabbard was never found.

Kjartan openly accused Bolli of being responsible for the loss of the sword and scabbard. Bolli disclaimed any knowledge of the affair. At this point the vindictiveness of Gudrun became so intense that nothing short of the death of Kjartan could appease it, and she openly encouraged her clansmen and husband to assassinate him. Gathering her husband, five brothers and friends together she sneeringly accused them of being afraid of Kjartan who was, she said permitted to go about insulting them with impunity. "Kjartan," she exclaimed, "may do things as boldly as he pleased, and no one dares to shoot a shaft at him." Then she calmly told Bolli that if he did not kill Kjartan she would refuse to be a wife to him.

The following year Gudrun's husband, brothers and retainers laid an ambush for the unsuspecting Kjartan as he was passing through a wood with a few friends. Kjartan on realising his danger sprang from his horse and valiantly defended himself against great odds, no fewer than five of the enemy attacking him at once. Although without the trusty sword the King had given him, he, Kjartan, proved too good for his attackers, though the sword he used was so poorly tempered that it kept bending and he had to straighten it with his foot. Bolli at first took no part in the fray, but stood by watching the attack; but when they found Kjartan's defence impregnable, one of the men appealed to Bolli to do something, even if it were to fight for Kjartan, whereupon Bolli, drawing his sword, joined in the assault. As soon as he did this Kjartan acted in a most unexpected manner: flinging away his sword he said that he would rather die than be guilty of injuring or killing his kinsman. Instead of admiring this generous act, Bolli, with much the spirit that characterised these old Vikings, calmly cut the unarmed man down, and then went behind him and supported him in his arms while he expired. It is said that Bolli immediately repented his dastardly deed, but such cruel and treacherous behaviour was common among these old Icelanders and was applauded rather than condemned. In those days the standard of fair play was exceedingly low. Gudrun, on hearing the news, expressed her delight and remarked that nothing pleased her more than to know that Hrefna would in future sleep alone. Bolli reprimanded Gudrun, and until his own untimely death—for he was shortly afterwards killed in a fight by having his head hewed off with an axe—he found no satisfaction in the death of his foster-brother. Poor Hrefna left her home afterwards and resided with her brothers in north Iceland, dying soon afterwards of a broken heart.

From this time on Gudrun showed herself to be a treacherous and murderous woman, doing her utmost to keep alive the feud between her own family and that of Kjartan and Bolli. She eventually married a third husband, Thorkell, who was accidentally drowned at the age of forty-eight. Gudrun is said to have felt the loss of this man so keenly that she repented and became deeply attached to the Church until she died.

Just before Kjartan's death a church had been built at Borg, near where Kjartan lived, and where these events took place, and his body was one of the first to be buried there. The full story of the life and death of Kjartan is told in the *Laxdaela Saga*, which gives an excellent insight into the social and economic conditions prevailing in Iceland during these early days of its colonisation. It is evident that these old Norsemen were wealthy, and although farmers for the main part, regarded the use of the sword and bow and arrow as worthy of all good men. Life was held very cheaply, and the slaughter was so heavy among the young men that one wonders how Iceland ever became populated. Doubtless they carried this warlike spirit over from Norway, where they had their origin. In course of time separation from the mother country caused them more and more to attend to the needs of their life at home, and more farming and less fighting became the rule; until today Iceland is without army, navy or air force.

CHAPTER 16

SOUTH BY ROAD

THE journey by car along the south coast showed me how deceptive the bird's-eye view from an airplane can be; and I have already stated how much I found I had missed during the airplane trip from Reykjavík to Budareyri. It flattened out the topography of the country to an amazing extent, and misled regarding both the population and arableness of this part of Iceland.

When Mr. Nikulas Fridriksson offered to motor me as far as Vatnajökull, I jumped at the chance, and returned from the journey after several thrilling days a wiser and happier man.

The fact is, much of Iceland's prettiest scenery lies along the south coast, which will always be sparsely populated unless the Government consents to make a harbour there. An extensive coast line with no harbour facilities is a grave drawback, and that is the unfortunate position. At Vík there is a natural coastal formation which, it is maintained, could easily be deepened and engineered into a presentable harbour. Should this be done it would be a safe prophecy that the south of Iceland would become more populous than the north, owing to its excellent farming and fishing facilities, as well as its milder climate.

The southern highway passes through Selfoss which is one of the most popular southern towns, situated on the Olfus about five miles inland from the sea. The river is spanned by the largest and handsomest bridge in Iceland, built by a British firm. Selfoss is a favourite resort for motorists from Reykjavík, which lies about thirty miles to the north-west.

The town is well supplied with hotels and restaurants, and as Selfoss is on the main route of long-distance motor 'buses, it is nearly always busy. After leaving Selfoss the traveller passes no important settlement until Vík is reached about seventy miles due east. Many historical landmarks are seen, however, including Hekla and the spot where Ingólfur Arnason lived previous to moving to Reykjavik. Before leaving Iceland I spent a pleasant Sunday in a pretty little summer house on the shore of Alftavatn, or "Swan Lake," nestling at the foot of Ingólfsjall, or "Ingólf's Mountain," named after the founder of the country who lived at one time close to it.

Looking towards the north as one journeyed along, was not unlike travelling through a fairyland, the mountains showing black and white against a cloudy sky. The clouds embraced the middle of the mountains and gave the impression that the peaks were floating in space. It was midsummer, and the surrounding country was grass-covered, adding charm to an already delightful scene.

There is plentry of farm land between Selfoss and Vík, and again and again the feeling of regret assailed our Canadian farmer, who still travelled with us, as she bemoaned the idle state of the soil, because of the lack of manpower. More and more the statement of one of the British Consuls—an Icelander—was pressed home upon me: "Iceland," he had said with conviction, "is capable of supporting a population of four millions." Our whilom Canadian could see nothing but potential wealth in every acre of grass-covered soil, and grew quite angry at the waste of such natural resources. There were, however, some large and prosperous farms scattered over a wide area, some of them centuries old, for this part of the country was one of the first to be settled.

On my way back from the east I was invited to dine at one of the most famous farms in this part of Iceland, the owner being a very influential man in the farming industry. His life had been spent in improving agriculture and he was ably supported by his son, a young man with whom I held a long conversation through an interpreter. This thoroughly up-to-date young man was not too hopeful about the productivity of the soil and thought that on the whole farmers had done the best they could. He had experimented with various crops in an endeavour to extend the scope, but had found it useless trying to grow oats, barley and corn generally as a paying proposition owing to something lacking in the soil. But he agreed that more green vegetables might be grown to advantage. This farm was a model of efficiency and had some particularly fine cattle, and some splendid ponies, which I saw tethered to railings. The farmhouse was a fairly modern building and made of concrete; the interior, furnished very simply, notwithstanding the owner being wealthy. He and his family were certainly hospitable and were loath to let me and my friends depart.

Farther on the highway crossed several wide streams, and being close to the sea they were at their widest and best. Some were glacier rivers, while others were mountainous in origin, the difference in the colour of their water standing out conspicuously. The snow and glaciers were melting rapidly in the bright sunshine of this unusually warm summer, and in consequence the rivers were very spirited.

Attempts have been made to turn the glacier rivers into farming use, but with disastrous results at Floi, where one of the first experiments of the kind was made. It needed experience to convince the irrigators that glacier waters could deposit too heavy a layer of mud on the land, and the experiment was eventually abandoned.

Near to these spoilt fields stood a pretty little white Lutheran church with a green roof, glittering in the sunlight. This church had a historical significance, being loaned once a year to the "Evangelists," a non-conforming body which originated from an English missionary who went to Iceland about forty years ago, to hold their annual Conference in. In most countries such an event would be of no importance, but in Iceland it made news and even history.

We crossed the famous river Thjorsá while it was in spate and a fine picture it made. The Thjorsá is a glacier river deriving its origin from Hofsjökull, a glacier situated almost in the geographical centre of Iceland. Tungufell-jökull and even Vatnajökull also contribute to its waters, which at the point where we crossed were deep and wide. Its beneficial influence on the surrounding country is obvious by the greenness and opulence of the soil; yet, strange to say, hardly a farmstead was to be seen for miles around!

The Westmen Islands had been in view almost from the moment we dropped from the elevated land west of Selfoss, and at this point, owing to our nearness to the coast and the clear atmosphere, they seemed but a few miles away. They consist of about a dozen islands, of which Heimaey is the largest. From a distance they looked uninviting from a habitable point of view, seeming to be little more than rocky eminences rising forbiddingly out of the sea. It seemed hardly possible that on more than one of them lived a not unprosperous people wringing their living from the sea, for apart from a little farming, fishing may be said to be the sole means of livelihood.

Although the Westmen Islands are an integral part of Iceland the inhabitants are regarded by those on the main-land much as Irishmen regard Englishmen, as a semi-alien race. On the whole the Westmen Islanders are different from the Icelander proper, having descended in part, some authorities maintain, from the Irish slaves who murdered Hjörleifur, the foster brother of Ingólfur. If so, something of their Irish ancestry seems to be depicted in their colouring, particularly in their darker hair. On the way we met a little Westmen Island boy of about twelve summers, grazing his shaggy pony. He was heavily clothed in fustian and was distinctly good-looking. His bearing was quiet and somewhat dignified as he talked with my Icelandic com-panions, in whose presence he was reserved but not shy. There is no desire on the part of Westmen Islanders to hide their origin; and those I have met have seized, I thought, the earliest opportunity to make plain from whence they came, lest they be mistaken for mainlanders. I had a walk and a talk with a Westmen Islander at Akureyri, where he was competing in the National Golf Championship, and he struck me as being very un-Norwegianlike, owing to his stocky figure and dark hair. He spoke almost perfect English and was extremely pleasant. Almost at once he informed me from whence he had come.

Soon after passing Thjórsa we came to Rangá, a non-glacier river, which was easily the largest and widest I had seen, although on the map it is shown as being much less impressive than Thjórsa. It is a mountain stream, its clear crystal-like water looking brilliant as it flowed rapidly towards the sea. Hereabouts there were no guest houses and we picknicked on the luscious Rangá Plains, a procedure I can heartily recommend to those travelling in mid-summer.

It was exactly at 1 p.m., on 30th July, that Eyjafallajökull came into view, scintillating from the top of its high mountain, and although several miles away it appeared to be quite close, so clear was the atmosphere. This is a most engaging glacier with its vast western tentacles sprawling down the mountain side like the arms of a mighty octupus, broken here and there by large masses of dark rock. This was the best view I had yet had of any glacier, and although only a small one, it is, by reason of its curious formation, worthy of note. When viewing it from the east and north it had looked like cream lying in a large basin.

Near here is the place where poor Gunnar Hamundarson lived the last of his brief life, and died. Although outlawed, like so many other exiled Icelanders, he refused to leave the land he loved so well. On his way to the sea with the intention of departing for Norway, he was so struck with the beauty of his surroundings that he stopped in his steps and cried: "Beautiful is this hill. I refuse to go farther." His decision was fatal. His unforgiving fellow countrymen and his enemies, on learning his intention, set out to destroy him. The story of his last stand has come down in history to the discredit of his wife, who thought more of her hair than of her brave husband's life. When run to earth Gunnar fought bravely until his bow broke and his wife refused to give him a lock of her hair to repair it. He still has the reputation of being the greatest athlete of his age, able to jump his own height when clothed in a suit of mail. His wife, whose memory is still execrated, was known by the curious name of Longpants.

The general outline of the coast is very rugged, but without deep bays, and every now and then the picture is enhanced by a stream or waterfall. We passed Skogarfoss, an exquisite waterfall and the biggest in the south. It consists of a single fall or drop from a great height and looked, in the bright sunlight, like a shimmering diamond with a million facets.

At this point Mýrdalsjökull, a fairly large glacier, appears, and, owing to the winding of the highway, it can be seen for several hours, so that it seems much larger than it really is. I learnt more about glaciers through skirting this one than I might ever have known, and their great power and destructive force becomes apparent when one sees the immense rocks they have torn from the mountains in their descent. They strew vast deposits of black sand and igneous rock for many miles in their irresistible flow. Near the western extremity of Mýrdalsjökull the roadway actually passes over one of these black sand-like desposits, and in some places the car had to make its own roadway. There is, however, little or no danger owing to the firmness of the deposit. The flow of water was terrific, and one river over which we passed was so treacherous that no less than eighteen deaths stand to its credit within living memory. These were due to the old pony method of fording, and will no longer bother Icelanders because a fine bridge has been built across the stream, which, however, can be fierce enough on special occasions to sweep it away unless great care is taken.

We were making for Dyrhólaey, or the Portland Head of Iceland, the southernmost part of the island; and later I climbed it along with three Icelanders, one of them a girl six years old. The rock rises precipitously from the shore and at first sight looks impregnable, but there are about two ways up from the west side, from whence we attacked it. It was my first experience in what may be termed real mountaineering, the pathway being broken and so steep that at times one seemed literally to overhang the sands below. However, once the top was reached the effort proved well worth while and we spent some time exploring the top of the rock.

On the summit stands a wireless station, and not far off to the south is a natural archway cut in the rock by the sea, through which on stormy days the sea bursts with tremendous noise and force. There were, too, some queer-looking birds with red heads and curved beaks which we approached close enough to photograph; but as soon as they discovered our presence they flew away.

The descent on the north side of Portland Head was much less dangerous than the ascent along the jagged trail, and to my amazement many sheep were peacefully grazing on extensive meadows. They must, of course, have climbed up as there was no farm on the rock.

Previous to making the climb we had spent some time at one of the old farms near to Portland Head, where resided my host's mother, and where he had been born and reared. The farm had been sold a short time before and the family were about to remove to Reykjavík, the old lady not having been so far from the farm during her long life of more than eighty years. This farmstead afforded a good example of the type of person Iceland farms produce. Mr. Nikulas Fridriksson had risen to be one of the heads of Reykjavík electrical department, while one of his brothers, who devoted his life to farming, and passed away through tuberculosis, won considerable local fame as a scholar and poet. We had tea with his widow at Vík and I was able to see his library and appreciate his wide intellectual interests. Today there is less likelihood of learning being in farms, owing to the greater interest the younger folk are taking in city life. In the old days a trip from Vík to Reykjavík took several days by pony and was an event indulged in only once or twice in a lifetime. Today, simply by catching the long-distance 'bus anyone can reach the capital in a few hours. There the attention of the farmworker is distracted from serious problems to the easier pleasure that the cinema, dance hall, and theatre can give. This is a genuine source of concern to the older members of these outlying communities who naturally incline to the opinion that their quieter and more leisurely way of living is the best. But this almost universal problem is not confined to the small settlements of Iceland.

At Vík I had been invited to lecture publicly and when I saw the little town straggling along the foot of the cliffs and up the hill side, I reconciled myself to the prospect of addressing a gathering consisting of myself, my friends and the local minister who was to act as Chairman. My surprise was great when I found the hall filled with an enthusiastic audience of over eighty. Practically every adult had turned out for the occasion, including the local Member of Parliament who was Sheriff of the district, and his family. After the lecture I had a long conversation with this gentleman, who gave me a good insight into the aims and objects of his constituents.

Vík is not more than fifty years old. It is a progressive community with big ambitions, for the inhabitants sincerely believe that in time a harbour will be made and Vík will become in a big way the principal centre of the south coast. The individual who knew most about this subject was the manager of the local co-operative stores, and he held forth on the prospects of south Iceland at considerable length and with force and logic. Vík cannot grow by farming only; it needs increased fishing facilities. He had himself been a fisherman and knew a great deal about the best parts of the sea for this purpose. Should the Government agree to build the harbour it would save fifteen hours sea-journey to Northern ports by making the voyage unnecessary. The sea off Vík is said to produce splendid herring. If this man's forecast of the future of south Iceland be as correct as his forecast of the weather, then it may be taken for granted that the harbour will be built. Exactly to the hour the weather changed from fine to stormy, as he predicted it would, and he gave me quite a learned discourse on clouds and winds in the course of his forecast.

On top of one of the cliffs I discovered a group of Nissen huts in which lived about thirty British airmen. They were thoroughly bored by their inactivity and were longing to return home. They took but little interest in the local inhabitants, although they occasionally played football with them.

We left Vík en route for Kirjubaejarklaustur, where we intended staying a day or two before going on to Vatnajökull; but there were arranged some interesting calls on the way for my edification. Along the coast lay several interesting landmarks, including Hjörleifshofdi, a rock in which Ingólfur and his foster-brother lived for a time after arriving at Iceland. It was here that Hjörleifur was murdered by his Irish slaves. Later on they moved farther east to Ingölshofdi. I have already said that exactly why these early settlers elected to live on isolated rocks, which look barren and unable to sustain life, I never heard explained although there must have been a good reason, for Ingólfur and Hjörliefur were by no means fools.

To attempt to describe the scenery beyond Vík would be useless as much of it baffles description. Some outstanding peculiarities, however, lend themselves to the pen. The valleys are excessively green; the mountains fantastic because of the erosive action of the glaciers. At one point both Mýrdalsjökull and Vatnajökull are in view at the same time, and both look like immense eggs sticking over the rims of giant egg-cups. It would be impossible to find anything more charming than the delicious valleys of Kerlingardalur. They give the impression of giants having paraded through them with paint brushes, splashing the most delightful colours—mainly green.

Some of the mountains are composed of a soft substance called móberg, in texture resembling soapstone. It is so pliable that it can be cut with a knife, owing, it is believed, to previous glaciers having softened the rocks by humidity. A close examination revealed móberg to be a mixture of

11. Helka erupting

stone and silt, and because of its softness time and weather have cut it into a thousand strange shapes. It is as soft as a carpet to walk on, as on it grows a mellow green moss right up to the edge of the glacier.

All this is offset by plains of black shingly deposits left behind by running streams which from time to time have been compelled to alter their course. Nothing can grow in these shingles.

On descending the mountain we passed close to one of the huts erected to shelter shipwrecked mariners, that I had first seen from the air. It was a neat little cottage, nestling cosily in a small inlet to shield it from the wind. It stood on the borders of an immense black-shingle plain. Near by Mýsdalsjökull had descended to one of the black shingle deposits which was comparatively new, having been made by the eruption of Katla in 1918. It takes six hours to cross this plain by pony, but less than an hour by car, having to drive slowly because there is no highway through the black "sand." Owing to its shiny nature the shingle casts mirages quite as clear and deceiving as those of the Sahara Desert. I could have sworn at one time that we were about to enter a wide stretch of sea water in which stood large rocks and here and there a boat well laden with passengers; but on approaching the spot nothing but black "sand" met the gaze.

Katla is actually in the glacier, Mýrdalsjökull, and when it erupted it modified the coast line considerably, causing the sea to encroach on dry land, while huge pieces of the glacier became detached and floated out to sea.

We visited Hemra, a fine farm owned by a schoolmaster, who welcomed us as if we were members of his family. This farm was situated in a lovely hollow among hills, with one side somewhat open to the sea. Small cataracts coursed down the hills and a purling stream ran pleasantly through the meadow. Hay-making had been in full swing here also, and we spent some of the sunny afternoon water-divining, most of the company being able to make the twig twist whenever it was held over subterraneous water.

12. Eastside of lake showing The Free Church, Reykjavik, and the lake at Reykjavik at evening time.

Our host was both a poet and singer, and insisted on accompanying us to Hvammur, a farm standing at the end of an adjoining valley and reached over an almost impossible cart track. Our car was unable to negotiate such trying territory, the route crossing open country, and, as we were soon to learn, passing through a river. This farm, one of the most isolated in the country, was connected by telephone, and after a longish wait a large lorry picked us up and took us to our destination. This lorry was, apart from ponies, the only way the farm could be reached, and it served a score of purposes, from conveying produce to the market, to acting as a 'bus for the local inhabitants. Hvammur was a new farm in an old location, one of the oldest down south. The original farm had been destroyed in 1918 by Katla, the lava gradually consuming the house so that a new one had to be erected. All around stood masses of lava, giving some idea of the fierceness of the eruption.

The farm stood on the banks of the Skaftá River which the car had to ford before reaching the homestead. The farmer and his assistants were delighted to meet us, as visitors were few and far between; and the welcome was all the warmer by virtue of the fact that nearly everybody was related to the farmer and his wife. The good wife spent her time loading the table with viands and pressing them shyly on her visitors. Although fifty-five years of age this lady had left her district only once, to visit Reykjavík, and admitted that she had no desire to go again.

On leaving Hvammur we started on the last leg but one of our journey, our objective being Kirjubaejarklaustur en route to Vatnajökull. This meant passing through Eldhraun, the largest lava deposit in the world. This amazing place has an area of 120 square kilometres, and I had heard many accounts of its ghastly appearance, but I was not expecting anything like what I saw. The lava fields at Mývatn and Dimmaborg should have prepared me, but when I saw Eldhraun I was shocked. It must be the most extraordinary scene of devastation nature has created. In ghastliness it certainly baffles the imagination. Pile upon pile of contorted lava meets the astonished eye. Hell could not, except that it be hot, present a more terrific scene; and Eldhraun once was hot, a burning molten mass, hissing like a mighty cauldron filled with burning venom!

Time has softened the horrid spectacle in one respect only—it has cooled the lava. But in place of fire it has put something equally striking—moss. Almost every particle of lava has become covered with a lichen, which in dry weather is sage-green-grey, but which under a fall of rain immediately becomes a vivid green as if by magic. This moss has softened the contours of the brown masses of burnt out rock but has, in consequence, imparted a sort of life to it, and it is this which strikes the emotions with abhorrence and consternation.

Before this coating of lichen grew upon it, the lava could not have been mistaken for what it is; today it seems to reek with elemental life, making the vast mass look like creatures, many of the lowest types in bestial torment, with hosts of shattered men, women and children trying in vain to escape from the agony that seems to afflict them. Eldhraun is a ghastly nightmare. My friends and I called out the names of the creatures these contorted figures called up in our imagination. There lay the twisted remains of petrified or struggling rats, sheep, turtles, eagles, sphinxes, lions, tigers, elephants, snakes, dogs, bears, anything and everything capable of registering pain in its most acute form. It seemed to represent every form of life from amoeba to man. It takes about an hour to motor through without stopping; but we frequently alighted the better to see and to take photographs.

On issuing from it on the eastern side a most peculiar topographical formation is seen, one which science has never, I understand, been able to explain. It consists of numerous hillocks covered with grass. There are said to be more than a thousand of these lofty mounds, each composed of lava, and when excavated the interior looks like a mass of cinder. One surmise is that they were formed by volcanic action at the bottom of the sea, which receded and left them exposed.

They extend to the west bank of the Skafta, which flows at this point into a mountain stream. The Skafta is a glacier river and quite milky in colour, while the mountain stream is crystal clear. Where they flow into each other, almost a line could be drawn between them, the crystal waters disappearing suddenly into its murky neighbour. These streams are full of trout and salmon-trout, and we could see the fish disappearing and reappearing from the glacier water into that of the mountain stream. Mr. Fridriksson and I did some fishing here, but the night was far advanced and the fish wary, so that we returned to the guest-house with empty baskets. This was vastly different from the result obtained by a young fisherman, who arrived the following morning with a catch of 126 trout, salmon-trout and salmon, all caught in nets.

On the western side of the Skaftá stands Kirjubaejarklaustur, the last guest-house on the south coast before Vatnajökull is reached. It consists of a group of buildings typically Icelandic in their plainness, at the foot of high precipitous hills. It looks very inviting after Eldhraun, and it was with a feeling of relief that we alighted, and later dined. We knew that there awaited us, when we resumed our journey, another big lava field; but after seeing Eldhraun we felt we could face anything.

The guest-house consisted of an old farm with some new but temporary-looking buildings recently attached. The accommodation was similar to that which prevails more or less in all Icelandic guest-houses; but perhaps this was less satisfactory than in most cases. However, since everybody was in holiday mood—there is no other reason for going to Kirjubaejarklaustur—one did not mind the uncarpeted floor of the small barrack-like rooms, sparsely furnished with two iron bedsteads, a couple of chairs and the usual insufficient pegs on which to hang one's clothes. There was no paper on the walls. This spartan bareness also characterised the dining-room in which everybody sat at long tables, and each was friendly with his neighbour. The food was plain but good, and, of course, fish was cooked as only

Icelanders can cook it—deliciously. I swear I never knew how nice fish, fresh and salt-water, could taste until I went to Iceland!

The history of this guest-house is interesting. The original founder, father of the present owner, I understand, charged his guests nothing; doubtless feeling, as so many Icelanders did in the days when communications were difficult, honoured by visitors who broke the monotony of the day and brought news from the outside world. The advent of the motor-car has altered all that, and it would require a millionaire to feed and house the many visitors who go every summer to this popular resort.

Close to the hostelry stand the ruins of an old church and graveyard, which are being carefully preserved because of another of those "miracles" one hears of in Iceland. It is a similar story to that of the little church at Reykjahlid, on the shores of Mývatn, but more dramatic. In this church, during the terrible eruption of Askja in 1783, the local inhabitants made their final stand, and when all seemed lost, including their own lives, the unexpected happened and saved them—they believed in answer to prayer.

As the lava rained down destroying farms, crops and cattle, the pastor, himself a farmer, gathered together in the church what remained of his little flock, and having assured the frightened and chastened people that the Almighty had brought this calamity upon them because of their sins, he prayed that their lives might be spared. All this time the lava was approaching the church from two directions, east and west. Should these two vast masses of molten lava meet, everything would be lost, and it seemed impossible to escape the danger. Yet the "impossible" happened. The western mass which had been flowing irresistibly towards the church, stopped dead on the banks of the Skaftá; and that on the eastern side was stayed also. We rode, when on our way to Vatnajökull right through the eastern field of lava as we had done through the western, and although it was not so impressive it was impressive enough. Nothing could have stood against the destructiveness of this molten mass any more than it could against the western field. The story becomes much more impressive when one stands on the site of the old church and looks across the river at the lava standing grimly on its banks as if regretting its unfinished work.

On 3rd August we left Kirjubaejarklaustur for Vatnajökull, only to find that the waters were flooding the rivers, making them unfordable, so that we reluctantly turned back. It is doubtful, however, whether we should have been able to approach near enough to Vatnajökull to have seen much more of the monster than we did from the farthest point that we reached. On the way we passed what I regarded as the most remarkably situated farmhouse that I have seen anywhere. It was built right in the midst of the lava beds, large boulders of igneous rock blocking even the way to the house. How anyone could have chosen such an unpropitious spot baffled even my Icelandic friends, and in the end we concluded that it must have been sentiment and not reason that had determined the decision. The house stood near a stream, and from it came a pretty girl carrying a water jug. She had evidently been to the river to fill it. There was also a boy standing by a shaggy pony, gazing meditatively at us.

No doubt in summer time these isolated folk saw human beings frequently; but during the winter months not even a neighbour would, I trow, have ventured through that disfigured country.

CHAPTER 17

ISLAND OF VIDEY

IN the bay to the north of Reykjavík lie several small islands, the most important of which is Videy, owned by Mr. Hafberg.

On several occasions Mr. Hafberg invited me to visit his home on Videy, but the weather was too rough to permit me to make the journey. The island lies about a quarter of a mile from the mainland, across a channel known as Videyjar Sund, and in fine weather the prospect is charming, but it becomes positively dangerous to attempt to cross in a small craft, such as Mr. Hafberg's motor launch, when a strong wind is blowing. Videy is exposed to the full force of the Atlantic ocean from the west, and at the best of times it is liable to breezes which greatly agitate the sea.

Towards the end of August, however, the weather permitted the trip and I was able to spend an enjoyable evening with Mr. Hafberg and his family. My host's extensive knowledge of the history of his country naturally added interest to the occasion.

In Icelandic poetry Videy is referred to as "the Pearl in the Channel." It is full of romantic history, while upon its shores were worked out political and commercial schemes which contributed a great deal to the prosperity of the country. Long before Reykjavík showed signs of becoming the capital of Iceland, Videy flourished as the seat of Government, being the property of the Crown. It was selected by the King of Denmark as the home of the Governor and of the Chief Justice, and at the beginning of the nineteenth century its land values far exceeded those of Reykjavík only three or four miles away, across the bay.

Previous to this it had for centuries been one of the strongholds of the Roman Catholic Church. In 1225, Augustinian monks built a monastery there, and made the island so sacrosanct that no layman was allowed upon it alive, although the monks welcomed them heartily enough when they were dead. Their aim was to make Videy a spiritual centre towards which all Icelanders in the south and west of the country could turn for consolation at a price. In this way these monks stored up wealth for themselves and wielded considerable authority until 1550, when the monastery was destroyed by fire and the power of the church broken.

The result of this monkish plan was to make Videy a veritable charnel house, and the visitor can feel pretty sure, when walking about the island, that beneath his feet lie the remains of Icelanders who lived their little day and paid to be buried in Videy. The monks made it a kind of national cemetery, and relied upon it as the principal source of their income. The interment was done in no slipshod manner, and whoever was buried on the island, if brought from the mainland, was assured a flattering ceremony and ritual.

It is quite thrilling to stand upon the rocky shore of Videy and see the particular landmarks associated with this practice. In the distance on the mainland can be seen Likatorfa, or "Corpse Plain," where the body was placed in position by the mourners for the monks to collect and take to the island. This they did in a rowing boat, solemnly carrying the casket with its contents to Líkhóll, a flat, rocky headland of Videy. From here it was carried to the chapel which no longer exists, and after appropriate formalities, was buried. All this, when the dues were paid, ensured the departed freedom from the pains and penalties of purgatory and hell.

The opulence of the monks cost them dearly, for no matter how sacred the spot was held by fellow Icelanders, pirates treated it with such contempt that from time to time they invaded it and robbed the monks of their wealth. On the whole the pirates did very well, but on one memorable occasion at least they received such a warm reception that they refrained from attacking it for a long time.

This was when some Dutch pirates landed on Videy and attacked the monks, who heroically defended their gold, goods and cattle. Matters were going very well for the pirates until they made the mistake of killing the son of the Abbot. This so infuriated the good man that he set about the marauders to such purpose that they fled after suffering heavy losses.

Centuries later Videy became the seat of the Danish Government and the home of Skuli Magnusson, who to this day is regarded, in many respects, as the greatest and best minister that Denmark ever had in Iceland. There stands upon a small hill close to Líkhóll and not far from the old Government house, which is named after the island and now the abode of Mr. Hafberg, a monolith erected in 1911, in memory of Skúli. This memorial was placed in position exactly two hundred years after the birth of this famous political reformer, who lived until 1794. It is about twelve feet high, and in its severity conveys something of the simple but straight mind of this fearless but diplomatic Governor.

Skúli Magnússon was, as his name shows, an Icelander, and by retaining the Icelandic spelling shows that he did not, as did so many other Icelandic ministers, despise his oppressed countrymen and adopt a Danish way of spelling his name. This feature alone will keep him honoured among his countrymen, while Chief Justice Ólafur Stephensen, will remain less respected because he altered his to Danish.

Videy must have proved an awkward place for those who had to go there to pay taxes, and it shows great lack of consideration on the part of the Government to have thus inconvenienced and even endangered the lives of the people who, to perform this duty, were obliged to row across the dangerous channel. Their admiration for Skúli made this onerous task somewhat lighter, for they realised that all his sympathy was with them, and that with consummate skill he worked for their benefit while faithfully serving the King.

Only his incorruptibility made this possible, and he

remains a splendid example of how even a politician and administrator can successfully hold the balance of power between two opposing forces with justice, when his motives are unselfish. Skúli's task was far from easy. At the time Denmark was at the height of her power and had Iceland well under her feet, thus proving that a country, too small to smother a dependency, can, nevertheless, fail to mother it. Both the Danish Government and Danish trade monopolists were in so secure a position that it seemed impossible that anyone could stop them from ruthlessly exploiting their victims, who through years of oppression had lost the Viking spirit of their ancestors.

Skúli Magnússon succeeded because of his insistence on imposing the law in as beneficent a manner as it would permit, while he so cleverly attacked the trade monopolies that he succeeded in breaking the power of the merchants and built a flourishing factory in Reykjavík. For this splendid service alone he would have deserved the title which still affectionately characterises him—"The Father of Reykjavík." An idea of the brilliance of this accomplishment can be formed when it is remembered that at the time Icelanders were compelled by law to sell their goods to specific Danish merchants, from whom in turn they had to purchase whatever goods they required. To refuse to purchase at the price fixed or to refuse to sell under the same law laid the Icelander open to a public flogging, and this was cruelly enforced.

Among the services Skúli rendered Iceland was the building of Government House on Videy, a long, white-washed building capable of accommodating from fifty to sixty people. The present owner continues the tradition started by the Augustinian monks by farming in the orthodox Icelandic style. In addition he runs a successful business in Reykjavík. The house is built entirely of Icelandic greystone, the first to have been constructed of this material. Previous to this innovation all buildings, large and small, were built either of stone and turf, or of wood imported from Norway. The venture was justified, for "Videy" stands almost as firm today as the day it was erected. The question of mortar to hold the stone blocks and bricks together, for a certain amount of brick seems to have been included in the structure, was very important, and simple as the matter appears to the foreigner, here again Skúli Magnússon scored an important point for his native land.

Hitherto, mortar had been dependent upon the importation of sand from Denmark, but Skúli proved that just as good mortar could be made by grinding Icelandic stone and mixing it with lime. This invention not only struck a blow at Danish trade with Iceland, but helped to revolutionise building; while at the same time it made Icelanders less dependent upon foreign imports, an invaluable factor for a country practically devoid of natural resources.

Close by the Old Government House stands one of the oldest churches in Iceland, erected in 1759; it, too, is built of stone, and inside is so quaint that it may well claim to be among the most remarkable churches in Christendom. Unfortunately there is nothing artistic about it, and any ultra-postimpressionist in art might well regard it as a masterpiece in its demand upon the imagination to fill in what may be called the missing links. Externally it might well pass for an old barn; inside it is the embodiment of crudeness. Most old Icelandic churches are alluringly crude, and give the impression that the worshippers were too poor to erect better churches, and perhaps too much taken up with the spiritual aspects of their faith to pay attention to outward and visible features.

It is capable of seating not more than fifty people, although at times it is visited by much larger congregations from the mainland for special services. It is full of rough beams, while the altar is in complete harmony with the primitive architectural plan, and for no apparent reason the interior has been painted red, blue and green, without any attempt at artistic decoration.

The "Videy" Government House is an excellent example of the simple architecture of two hundred years ago. It shows the simplest planning, while evidently the architect's aim was to make every foot of the interior serviceable. It is three stories high, the upper storey being nothing more than numerous attics with small, unattractive rooms leading out of the main compartment, which was used for storing grain and other agricultural products. How they succeeded in keeping the place warm in winter must remain a mystery, and one can only conclude that those who were obliged to sleep in the upper attics—and it was here that most of the farm hands slept—must have suffered greatly in severe weather. During the early part of the Danish rule there was a good deal of class distinction enforced by the Danish authorities who are said to have despised Icelanders, and mixed with them only so far as necessity compelled. Today it is different, and here I found the daughters of the owner sharing their bedrooms with the female farmhands.

Ólafur Stephensen, an important administrator and judge, a contemporary of Skúli Magnússon, appears to have resided in the Government house at the same time as his famous compatriot. Stephensen figures quite often in books of travel written by eminent Britishers about the early part of the nineteenth century, and he seems to have left a deep impression on their minds by his ostentatious and oppressive hospitality. He was a stickler for Danish etiquet in the entertainment of his guests, which should not be mistaken for Icelandic, as few, if any, Icelanders of that day could have fed stray visitors so well. He succeeded Skúli but never won the admiration of Icelanders who, to this day, regard him as something of a renegade.

Several other important personages made "Videy" their abode for longer or shorter periods, among them being Eggert Ólafsson, a noted farmer, author and poet with a definite scientific bent. He travelled through Iceland during Skúli's time, endeavouring to find the best way to farm, as well as to study geological formations in the hope of doing something useful for trade. A close friend of Skúli's, he often made "Videy" his resting place while composing his poems and writing in the interests of his beloved country.

Then there was Bjarni Palsson, the first Icelandic medical

doctor. He eventually married one of Skúli's daughters, and often made "Videy" his temporary home. It was such men as these, clever, fearless and enthusiastic for the best interests of their native land who paved the way for the great political reformer, Jón Sigurjonsson.

It was agreeable to gaze upon the scenes which so long before had delighted the eyes of these Icelandic notabilities; and it was not difficult to realise something of the emotions that filled their breasts when looking upon the rich pastures and splendid seascapes of this charming little island. Videy is so situated that a hundred different and engaging scenes please the eye. Fortunately for me my visit was in the evening and at a time when the midnight sun had not entirely ceased to lighten the skies. By gazing westward one was sure to catch the brilliant hues cast by the declining sun, and to see the mountains bathed in some of the most startling and lovely colours of the spectrum.

Henderson, writing about his visit to Videy during his residence in Iceland at the beginning of the nineteenth century, spares a few words for Videy, which he visited and enjoyed. He speaks of the large number of eider-ducks "that annually frequent" the island, and emphasises what I cannot endorse after seeing both places; its superiority "to any other spot in the southern parts of the island." But it need not be less elegant for not surpassing, or even equalling some of the charms of southern Iceland; it is beautiful enough to please anyone who loves nature and pastoral scenery. I shall long carry in my memory the peaceful scene that characterised that little landscape: the ploughman homeward plodding his weary way; the cattle calmly grazing on the luscious grass; the sheep wandering over the little hills and in the pretty dales, while at the north end of the island one could see the remains of an old and disused fish-curing station.

The rock-bound shore revealed how almost inaccessible the island was, and the skeletons of many a ship lie hidden beneath the waves; for Videy can be treacherous. Towards the end of the recent Allied occupation a terrible accident happened to some American soldiers who had ventured to embark in boats in the bay. Night overtook them, a storm arose, and practically all of them were drowned off the least hospitable part of Videy. All this tragedy seems in keeping with the birth of this famous little isle, which was vomited up by volcanic action from the depth of the sea.

CHAPTER 18

RETURN TO REYKJAVIK

WE returned to Reykjavík, after our futile attempt to reach Vatnajökull, in time to spend August Bank Holiday there. It may be mere coincidence that causes Icelanders to make the first Monday in August their main summer holiday. It certainly made me feel more at home.

With the exception of a visit to Hafnarfjordur, a fishing town of considerable importance six miles south of the capital. I spent the remainder of my stay in Iceland mainly in Reykjavík, with occasional visits to places of interest not too far away.

I lectured in Hafnarfjordur in the Free Church, there being only two churches of this persuasion in the country. There is no difference in doctrine and teachings between the Free Church and the Lutheran.

Hafnarfjordur is built almost entirely on the side of a hill of lava, overlooking the harbour. It is amazing that this rugged material can have been levelled sufficiently to build so many delightful houses on it. But every now and then nature has proved too obstinate and masses of lava project threateningly between the residences, producing a very curious effect. The main thoroughfare is said to be the best paved in the entire country.

Soon after my return I paid a visit to Álafoss, a small garden city, as individualistic as its owner, Mr. Sigurjón Pjetursson. This gentleman had already placed me under a great obligation by motoring me to Great Geysir and Gullfoss, and now he took me to see the woollen mills of Álafoss and the communal way of living there. The entire staff, including the proprietor's two sons, live on this estate which is fully equipped with practically every necessity, including a poultry farm. It has a fine open-air swimming pool as well as an inside warm one; and an open-air theatre with terraced seats.

Reykjavík in August and September was warmer than in June and July, and the city more attractive because flowers were in full bloom. The inhabitants of the capital are lovers of nature, and whenever possible grow plants, even trees, in their gardens, and some of them become quite imposing. Every kind of plant that will grow in volcanic soil has a chance, and in consequence the grey concrete of the houses is relieved by a veritable galaxy of colour. As far as I could judge, every flower that adorned these gardens was common to Britain, including peonies, tulips, marigolds, pansies, wall-flowers and stock.

One of the places where flowers grow in profusion is the old cemetery on the hill side overlooking the lake which is one of Reykjavík's chief attractions. Looking eastward from it the city appears very like a doll's town, with its coloured roofs and houses. Here stands the upright stone which marks the resting place of Jón Sigurdsson, the national hero; while around this unpretentious monument lie the graves of many of Reykjavík's whilom leading citizens.

A new cemetery has just been made outside the town, in which lie buried soldiers, sailors and airmen of several of the allied nations who fought together in the World War. Upon these serried rows of crosses are inscribed the names and rank of those who lie beneath. It is depressing to find that death has failed to be recognised for the leveller that it is, great care having been taken to distinguish the graves of officers and padres so that they may not be confused with the rank and file. One would have supposed that since all died for the same cause, death would at least have been permitted to demonstrate liberty, fraternity and equality.

Some original tombstones are to be found in this graveyard, the most impressive being one dedicated to an unknown sailor; indicative of the regard in which members of this occupation are held in Iceland.

I now had ample leisure to browse round the city and take in its principal features, and found the docks and harbour a constant source of interest. The harbour was an amazing revelation of the activity and prosperity of this little nation. On one occasion I counted more than twenty vessels, many of them quite large, anchored there, most of them taking in or discharging cargoes. It seemed bizarre that 130,000 people could cause so much mercantile commotion, and the sense of wonder was increased when it was remembered that at Akureyri in the north, other large ships would also be lying; while at the smaller towns like Husavik and Eskifjördur many fishing vessels would be found. It was still remarkable even when due allowance was made for the demands of the American service men still in Iceland; but by now their numbers were inconsiderable. Iceland was clearly a hive of industry.

From time to time the British ships of war put into the harbour. On one occasion a fleet of sixteen minesweepers helped to fill the harbour and bay, their crews swelling the crowds always to be found in the main thoroughfares of Reykjavík. A good many American ships of war also came and went, and the different ways of their crews showed that, although they spoke the English language, they did not behave like Britishers. They were, as a rule, much more friendly and noisy. On one occasion a large boat from an American warship landed a number of sailors, including two negroes who were evidently practising for a vaudeville show. Immediately they were on shore they seized the opportunity of doing their dance-steps along the jetty to which their boat was tethered, and excellent dancers they were. Not the slightest self-consciousness afflicted them, as with uproarious laughter and loud singing they performed their dance with great precision. Often these American boats brought mixed crews of white and coloured sailors ashore, and although I watched them closely there was nothing to indicate that there was a colour bar.

Reykjavík is almost a model of social services, and has a home for aged people that must be one of the most comfortable in the world. I spent quite a pleasant afternoon in it, visiting the sick and talking with some of the inmates. Old-age must have lost its dread for those who know that when everything else fails they can enter this retreat. The home contains some interesting personalities; one of them, a retired schoolmaster who spent several years in Canada and the United States, was particularly interesting, and he discoursed with zest about his experiences abroad. But the call of Iceland had proved too strong and in his old-age he had returned to the city of his birth, and there awaited his end, (which occurred in February, 1947), full of the activity for the cause he loved, which is that of a voluntary colporteur.

Talks with old Icelanders whose memories go back to the bad old days, when life was arduous and want prevalent, were illuminating. Their stories clearly indicated the extreme poverty that once afflicted these people, at a time when nobody was really rich. They told of fishermen who laboured all day and all night, returning to their homes for a few hours only to hurry to sea again. It was work, work, work for a mere pittance. There is still evidence of their poverty in the poor houses they dwelt in; little cottages, crudely built, and incapable of lasting much longer. The Reykjavík of today is like another world, so superior is it, and every week makes it better as the various ambitious building schemes develop.

It seems incredible that forty years ago this place was practically devoid of proper sanitation, and that to procure water people had to walk to the centre of the city carrying two buckets hanging from a wooden support across the shoulders. At that time there were several wells in Reykjavík, and a practising professor of water clocks! Until 1905, practically nothing had been done to bring the city up-to-date, no buses, no trains, no trams; all transportation being done by ponies, with the exception of a few unattractive, small chars-a-bancs with temporary covers and often open sides, each capable of holding about eight people. Iceland then was about the least developed civilised country in the world, although it always managed to keep up with Europe and America in its styles of clothes. Old pictures of Iceland, especially of Reykjavík, which was always in advance of the rest of the country, reveal a city of old farms and crude dwellings, peopled by men, women and children garbed, for the most part, after the manner of British workmen of that period. Occasionally, however, the streets would be embellished by a gentleman strolling along, wearing a tall silk hat and carrying a walking-stick or umbrella.

They were then much less like their Viking forebears than today—a fact more than once commented on by visitors who must have been disappointed by their uncouth appearance. Whatever adornment they had was in their minds rather than on their backs, a fact also often noticed by early travellers. One author, commenting on this, suggests that it is a mistake to identify the modern Icelander with the early Viking founders of the country, whom he likened to Kilkenny cats. They consistently slaughtered each other, their slaves surviving them and thus forming in large part the population of today. No Icelander would, of course, care to endorse this theory, although there may be something in it.

An idea of the improvement that has taken place within recent years can be formed by the expensive preparation travellers to Iceland had to make as recently as 1930. Today anyone can go to this island without in any way altering his wardrobe. I took with me nothing more than I wear every day in Britain. Twenty years ago called for a special outfit, including riding breeches, oilskin trousers, a sou'-wester, warm flexible gloves, a tent, sleeping-bag and a compass. To carry food, most of it in air-tight tins, was a necessity; and, of course, there were the inevitable ponies—one to ride and another to carry one's pack. The whole arrangement resembled preparations for an arctic expedition.

To read the accounts of travellers in Iceland at even the beginning of the twentieth century shows what hardships they suffered through exposure to bad weather; it often took many days to travel journeys which now take only a few hours. What a difference there is between entering a modern automobile or motor bus—which travels, as a rule, faster than a private car—and having to prepare as "For a party of seven, plus two guides, we needed seventeen horses, riding nine, five pack and three spare."

Perhaps no country has been described in more contradictory terms than Iceland, so that anyone desirous of knowing the truth should visit it themselves. As recently as 1936 the authors of *Letters from Iceland* assure us that "Icelanders are all sick in buses." This suggests that in some unaccountable way Icelanders are different from other mortals, the vast majority of whom can ride in buses without such inconvenience. I travelled hundreds of kilometres in buses and met no Icelander who was sick, but observed that they so enjoyed this mode of travelling that they often spent their time in the vehicle singing heartily.

Mrs. Oswald stated that to be "alone in Iceland you are alone indeed." I have visited twenty-seven countries, and in many of them travelled extensively, meeting large numbers of natives, but in none of them did I encounter more friendliness nor feel so little alone as in Iceland.

Another writer informs us that "Nowhere a single tree appears which might afford shelter." The fact is there are several extensive forests in Iceland, but few big trees. An entirely different fact.

Speaking of Reykjavík, Henderson says, "Reykjavík is, unquestionably the worst place in which to spend the winter in Iceland. The tone of society is the lowest that can be imagined . . . it is totally devoid of intellectual gratification." A statement so far from the truth that in this land where one hundred per cent. of the population are literate, and where reading, writing and story-telling have always prevailed among the total population, Reykjavík always was the principal cultural centre. I can speak from personal experience so far as my visit is concerned, by saying that in no other capital city have so large a percentage of the population attended my lectures, and they were all on serious subjects. Over a period of fourteen weeks the interest was consistently sustained, and at the last lecture, although a special hall had been engaged, it was filled to capacity half an hour before the advertised time, and scores of people failing to gain admission.

Perhaps Horrebrow reaches the zenith of misrepresentation when he states, "They are not robust and hardy that nothing can hurt them; for they are human beings and experience sensations common to mankind." A subtle suggestion that Icelanders are not quite human. The truth is they are among the most robust and good-looking people in the world. So full of "sensations" that they are extremely sensitive, easily hurt, kindly, humorous and generous to a marked degree. Their reserve often arises from good manners and perhaps a slight inferiority complex, due to the realization of their national weaknesses in a world where only strong and warlike nations are regarded as truly "great."

Burton assures us that they have "eyes cold and dour—cold as pebble," an opinion somewhat offset by Von Troil, who regarded them as "of a good honest disposition; but they are at the same time so serious and sullen that I hardly ever remember to have seen any of them laugh." At that time this was understandable, for the country was then extremely poor, without fuel, and silently suffering under the severe and unjust rule of a callous conqueror. McKenzie found them to be a "poor but highly respectable people," which is a brief but accurate summary of the truth. But Pfeiffer tells us that, "If I attempted to describe some of their nauseous habits, I might fill volumes," and, according to Annandale, "their culture was squalid." The women fared at the hands of critics no better than the men. Hooker refers to the "grotesque appearance" of the Icelandic men who boarded his ship. Another writer, commenting on the women, informs the world that, "Among the gentler sex a soft look is uncommonly rare, and the aspect ranges from a stony stare to a sharp glance rendered habitual by a fiercer frown."

It is, of course, unnecessary to criticise these adverse accounts, some of which are so extreme that common sense instantly dismisses them as the outcome of unjust bias.

The description, for instance, of Icelandic women is so unnatural that one marvels how any intelligent person could bring himself to write it. In common with most Scandinavian women, with perhaps the exception of Danish, the Icelandic are reserved until properly acquainted with anyone. Then they show all the pleasant traits attributed to the fairer sex at their best. I met scores of them in private as well as in public life, and came to regard both sexes as polite, friendly and understanding. It is a grave pity when good manners are mistaken for vices, but the danger is prevalent, as I found when talking to those British sailors on the minesweeper, when they accused the Icelanders of the very defects which characterised themselves, which, in effect, arose from shyness and national conceit. Powerful nations always incline to look down on weak ones.

While on this subject of the different reactions of visitors, a further example may be mentioned in regard to Iceland's natural phenomena. Henderson refers to the spiritual upliftment that he felt while watching Great Geysir, but Darwin called it an "old brute!"

Icelanders must waver between amusement and indignation at these contradictory accounts. They have a proverb to the effect that, "He is a friend who tells you of your faults," and another which maintains that "Ale is another man." The latter proverb must afford them some consolation when they read of a notable scientist who visited them and referred to their "nastiness and stench." A sober man could hardly say such a thing. If it were true at the beginning of the nineteenth century, it is certainly quite untrue of today.

That Icelanders are among the most tolerant of people is demonstrated by their religious attitude. They have never lost the sound commonsense that characterised Thorgeir, the old pagan who decided whether Pagan Iceland should embrace Christianity. After serious cogitation in solitude he pronounced his decision from the Rock of Laws at Thingvellir; a splendid compromise, which permitted the introduction of the new faith because he wanted to avoid civil war.

Commonsense was further shown by the new converts, equally anxious to stay the destroying hand of Olaf Tryggvason, who was determined to force Christianity upon them or exterminate them. After Thorgeir's decision they had to be baptised, and finding the waters of the Oxará too cold, rode away to the nearest hot springs to be baptised there. It is a unique feature of Iceland that it underwent compulsory conversion to a foreign faith without spilling one drop of blood.

This spirit of religious compromise has never died out, and is as obvious today as in the year 1000. Although the Lutheran church is a national church, every priest in it deriving his income from the state, and therefore under state control so far as religious discipline and doctrines are concerned, it holds most tolerant views. One outstanding feature is the strong sympathy the leaders of the Church show towards psychical research. In lecturing on this subject throughout the country practically all my public meetings were arranged by the local priest, who invariably took the chair for me after having announced the meetings from his church pulpit.

There is, of course, a reason for this attitude, summed up briefly by a recent Icelandic writer to the effect that ancestor worship has always played a part in the religion of the Icelander. It is certain that the old Vikings firmly believed their gods visited the earth from time to time in human form, and that Valhalla was an abode in which the hero would meet his forefathers.

There is still felt considerable respect for the ancient god Thor. Place-names show this popularity, while some of Iceland's leading citizens have adopted it as a name in some form or other. There remains also the tendency to honour this god by opening the sessions of the Althing on Thursday, the day named after him. It was Thor who was supposed, above all other gods, to have directed Ingólfur Arnarson's house pillars to where Reykjavík now stands, just as he was believed to have directed Helgi the Lean, through oracles, where to land when he came in sight of Iceland. Even after

Christianity had been established, the power of Thor was invoked to resist undesired encroachments of the new faith, sometimes by direct challenge between Thor and Christ. There is no doubt that Iceland benefited by the adoption of Christianity, however, as within six years of its establishment as the national faith duelling, which had been so prolific in the spilling of some of Iceland's best blood, was prohibited.

A generation or so ago perhaps most Icelanders believed in the existence of nature spirits, and regarded them as able to influence human life for good or ill. Even today the belief is by no means dead, and I met people who sincerely believed that elves were able to influence people through dreams. Icelandic elves are not only human in appearance but very human in many of their habits. The idea was that these aerial creatures lived in the same localities as human beings and adopted a similar mode of livelihood. Thus any farm might have its elfin counterpart although invisible to the normal eye. Elves were supposed to have the power to assume human form by making themselves visible, and this they did either to render a service or to do an injury.

In Reykjavík, I was assured that a well-known midwife who lived about thirty miles to the north-west, and who was famous for never having lost a patient or child, obtained her remarkable ability through an elf. This case is worth recording as it gives a comprehensive idea of the popular beliefs about the character and doings of these nature spirits.

This particular lady, when a young woman, had a dream in which an elf man is supposed to have requested her to go with him to deliver his wife of a child. The dreamer explained that she would be useless as she knew nothing of midwifery; but the elf assured her that she would do all right. On consenting to accompany him, she found herself out of her body and walking across the farm to a hill nearby, on which she was surprised to see a farmhouse surrounded by aerial fields corresponding with those of the farm on which she lived.

The elf took her into this farmhouse and she noticed

everything resembled a normal Icelandic homestead. There was an old woman spinning, a fire in the grate, and in a normally furnished bedroom she found the expectant mother. The child was safely delivered and after the elf woman had been made comfortable with her newly born child the woman expressed the wish to return home. The elf man conducted her back to her bedroom, thanking her sincerely for the efficient way she had aided his wife. "I can, of course, give you no money," he said, "but I can help you in another way. Henceforth you will be an expert midwife and you will never lose a patient or a child."

I was assured that this promise came true; that the young woman, without so much as one lesson in the art of midwifery, became a most successful obstetrician and never lost a case. Her memory is still revered, and many tales are told about her remarkable ability.

Dreams are very popular in Iceland and I can testify to the firm belief in them still prevailing. Indeed, while I was in Reykjavík a number of these night visions were recounted to me by well-known people who were themselves the dreamers, and it was obvious that they had no doubt that by this means they were able to obtain useful information of prognosticatory character. Perhaps one of the most extraordinary was connected with a little Indian idol that was shown to me. The lady who claimed to have had this strange experience was well-known to me, and I can testify to her intelligence.

One night she dreamed that a Hindu priest came to her and after a conversation told her that as a guarantee of the genuineness of his presence he would give her, as a present, an idol of one of the Hindu gods. He then handed to her the metal image and on awakening she found it clasped firmly in her hand! It was a small image made of a bronze-like metal and was solid and real.

I met both persons connected with the following mysterious affair, the dreamer being a well-known trainer of athletes and sportsmen in Reykjavík; the afflicted young man a government official with a University education.

Years ago a young woman in Iceland committed suicide by cutting her throat. The reason for her terrible deed was well known: she had, for ten years been housekeeper to a Lutheran priest and during that period his mistress also. He suddenly abandoned her and married another woman, the shock of this causing the young woman to take her own life. It was the custom in Iceland to bury suicides in unconsecrated ground; in consequence the body of this unfortunate woman was buried outside a churchyard.

The priest responsible for the poor woman's action showed some remorse by inscribing her name in the church register, an act contrary to church regulations. He was subsequently murdered by some men who resented his behaviour to the dead woman, his body, it is believed, having been thrown down a crevasse and never recovered. Some years after these events another priest officiating at the church struck the name of the suicide from the church register, on the grounds that its presence there was illegal.

Nothing unusual happened for several years after this; then this priest's daughter-in-law gradually became mentally unbalanced and was ultimately confined in a lunatic asylum, where she eventually died. The onset of her disorder was very subtle, fits of insanity being followed by periods of sanity, no one knowing the cause. While this unfortunate woman's body lay awaiting interment, the gentleman who told me the story had a dream during which the spirit of the dead woman seemed to come to him begging him to see that she was not buried "with that woman." The apparition was in very great distress and obvious fear. The dreamer, anxious to render any assistance he could, enquired the name of the woman to whom she referred. She admitted that she did not know much about her, but gave the name of the suicide who had died so long before. Furthermore, the apparition stated that her body was to be placed in the casket the following day, a fact unknown to the dreamer, and she earnestly requested him to see that she was buried lying on her left side in the coffin.

On awakening, the dreamer, who had had very good reason to respect his dreams, recalled vividly every detail of this one, and telephoned to the husband of the dead woman, enquiring when the body of his wife was to be placed in the coffin, and was informed that it would be on the morrow, thus proving one item at least of the dream to be correct. He then recounted to the husband his dream, stressing the wish expressed by the apparition that she be placed on her left side when in the casket. The husband readily consented to do this, stating that he recalled that some time before her death his wife had made a similar request of him. The only reason he could think for this was that his wife had always slept on that side.

The dreamer informed me that he attended the funeral, and everything went off without a hitch. But soon after the interment one of the deceased woman's sons became mentally disturbed, declaring that every now and then he felt as if someone was trying to strangle him. So persistent became this persecution that he refused to sleep alone and insisted on occupying the same bedroom as his brothers. This, however, brought no relief. One day he appeared at the house of the dreamer and told him of his predicament, begging him to allow him to sleep in his bedroom as he had a feeling that this would relieve him of his obsessions. His surmise proved correct, but when he slept elsewhere the feeling of strangulation returned.

About this time the dreamer made the acquaintance of an automatic writer living in the city who had frequently proved that she could, by this means, obtain correct information unknown to anyone, and he asked her to interest herself in the young man's case. She did so, and received an automatically written message purporting to come from the young woman who had committed suicide, in which she begged that her bones be disinterred and reinterred in consecrated ground, naming the cemetery in which she wished this to be done. It was a considerable distance from the churchyard outside of which her bones were supposed to have been buried. They had, however, been deposited elsewhere, and, said the automatic writing, only two men in the country knew the whereabouts of the coffin.

Further information was forthcoming stating where the body was, and on this being conveyed to the obsessed young man, he undertook to carry out the wishes of the suicide. He personally informed me how he found the two men who showed him the coffin in which the remains of the unfortunate young woman lay, and on opening it removed from it a small religious relict which he showed me, and which he had reason to believe had been secretly placed in the coffin by the priest who had caused her to commit suicide.

All the facts of this strange case were placed before the Lutheran Church and permission was given for the reinterment of the body in the cemetery mentioned in the automatic writing. Thereafter the young man found himself free of his obsession. The point of view taken by the persons intimately related to the extraordinary affair, namely, the dreamer, the young man, and the automatist, is that the poor suicide had been "earth-bound" since her death by the fact that her body had not been buried in consecrated ground that she obsessed the poor woman who had died because she had been related to the priest who had erased her name from the church register; and when she died, transferred her venom to her son.

They believe also that the suicide had another object in view, one worthy of the imagination of Edgar Allan Poe—if she could possess the body of a living person, she hoped that she would be able to retain it until the body was buried in consecrated soil.

CHAPTER 19

ODDS AND ENDS

EVERYTHING of supreme national importance is, of course, to be found in Reykjavík, and to it we must look for the greatest signs of progress. The future policy of the country is being formed there, and there will be found the principal national driving force. Anyone dining at the Sjalfstaedishus (Conservative Club) is almost sure to see some of the leading politicians any day. There is nothing standoffish about these men, who will give a smile and nod to the stranger from abroad, not the least friendly of them being Mr. Ludvik Hjalmtysson, the genial Manager of the restaurant. Here I dined frequently partly because of the good service and partly because of the good company.

Reykjavík is also the centre of education, although, because of the high regard in which learning has always been held, there are excellent schools all over the country. The first schools were founded in the eleventh and twelfth centuries, and in them was taught a variety of subjects, mostly religious. A century or so later they suffered a decline; but the fact remains that many Icelanders could read and write when those arts were unknown to vast numbers in Europe.

Reykjavík University, a very handsome building in severe style, standing on the outskirts of the city, was founded in 1911. It has a very good medical school which was established as early as 1876, and has done such yeoman service that since its installation the statistics of the decline of disease are quite startling. Owing to bad housing the death rate in Iceland was terrific, infant mortality being appalling; symptomatic of the prevalence of disease generally. Scarcely any children survived in the Westmen Islands between 1790-1810. Most of them died in one week or less, few survived three weeks. The mortality among mothers was correspondingly high. Death of women from child-birth is now only 3.5 per thousand, and the death rate among children one of the lowest in the world. One hundred and forty years ago there were only three hospitals in the entire country; today there are more than forty.

Tuberculosis has been got well under control, and about four years ago there was a round-up of unsuspected cases through compulsory examination, the patients being drafted into the large sanatorium at Vifilstadir, a few miles outside Reykjavík. I received an invitation to lecture before the inmates of this State Institution, and when I arrived the lecture hall was crowded with interested men and women, most of whom were young, only a few showing signs of their dread disorder.

Reykjavík also has a very well-equipped National Medical Research Laboratory, and under the guidance of Mr. Kári Petursson I spent a most interesting afternoon inspecting the buildings, which contain the Medical Museum, and examined through the microscope some specimens of tubercular and leprosy germs. It is believed that these germs are related because they take the same stain. Their appearance, however, is different, the tubercular germ being spiral, while that of leprosy is flat and amorphous. British and American military medical officers were astonished at finding such a splendidly equipped laboratory in this out of the way part of the world.

Iceland has no public art gallery and pictures are relatively few. Art, however, is well represented in both old and new styles, while there is a growing demand for canvasses by leading native artists, for Iceland is quite art-conscious. Scattered throughout the country, usually in old churches, are to be found some very old paintings, generally of religious subjects, and all more or less crude. The few in the National Museum adjoining the National Library in Reykjavík are not much better.

Only two Icelandic sculptors appear to have been outstanding and both won world renown. One is the famous Albert Thorvaldsson who died in 1844, a specimen of whose work is to be seen in Reykjavík Cathedral. He is usually regarded as a Danish artist, his father only being an Icelander, and he is said to have been born at sea on the way to Denmark, but this is disputed.

The other is Einar Jónsson, whose private residence is also an art museum which, when he passes away, will revert to the State that built it and retains Jónsson as curator, granting him a pension. The arrangement works very well, and speaks volumes for the acumen of a Government which recognises a genius and found this excellent way to inspire his talent and retain his works.

I spent a thrilling morning with him and his wife, and left feeling that I had been in the presence, not only of a great artist, but also of an outstanding personality. Einar Jónsson's main objective is to glorify Iceland and express in imagery what may be termed her "spirit," especially her pioneer spirit. He has certainly done some remarkably fine things as a result of these ideals. His work combines originality, power, and spiritual beauty. It is almost entirely after the classical Greek style, his expressions invariably being noble, as in the case of Ingólfur Arnarson which stands on a small hill near the National Library, Reykjavík.

Some of his work is indescribably subtle in treatment and meaning, since most of his subjects are of a mystical and symbolical nature. He may be said to have immortalised Iceland in stone, and has "created something new on a national basis." Gazing at these marvellous carvings and listening to an explanation of the ideas that gave rise to them, one feels that the very spirit of ancient Iceland broods over these glorified stones. The result of the visit was to increase my admiration for the early pioneers who came and conquered one of the most unpropitious-looking countries in the world, and made it a vital living thing—the modern Icelandic Republic. No one is better able to understand the relentless will and untiring persistence of the Viking forefathers of this people than Einar Jónsson, That he has no message for the modern artist who follows the example of Cezanne, Picasso and Matisse, can easily be understood.

I made the acquaintance of two young Icelandic artists in Reykjavík. Both progressive, especially Mr. Kjartan Gudjonsson, an art teacher as well as a painter. He has strong views on art and favours the school of Picasso and Matisse. In his opinion true art must express the artist's own personality; mere imitators of schools naturally contribute nothing to the progress of art.

Mr. Gudjonsson's work finds a ready market in America where the ultra-modern in art is highly valued. One of the reasons for his success is that he is not an extremist. His latest picture at the time I was with him was proof of this. It depicted two fishermen representing Iceland. In painting it he aimed at simplicity of form and colour, basing the drawing on the cubist principle. Both figures were crude and heavy because fishermen are crude and heavy; he used plain colours, in blue, brownish-red and yellow-grey because they emphasised the simplicity of the subject. There is little that is æsthetic about fishing.

The other artist, Mr. Halldor Pjetursson, struck me as being a fine expressionist, with simplicity of form, colour, and composition, and with considerable strength. He often specialises in animals, particularly in Icelandic ponies, with great success. By no means a serious abstractionist, he nevertheless succeeds in conveying much of the underlying principles of his subject, but none of them were so abstruse that they could not be understood. His ponies, for example, had a solidity about them that showed not only the strength and endurance of these little animals, but also their stolid patience.

There is no Icelandic school of art, although the topography of the country naturally affects the artist's work. The best example of this is Kjarval, a painter as outstanding in his field as Einar Jónsson is in his. Kjarval is so popular that he has become a fashion and everybody who can afford to pay high prices will purchase one of his pictures and hang it conspicuously. Landscapes are his favourite subject; at least, I do not remember seeing any other kind of exhibit from his brush. He is something of an impressionist and always stimulating if one likes mountainous scenes in dark and lurid colours. There must be something very appealing about his work to Icelanders who speak of him with great admiration and almost bated breath. I saw him while at Kirjubaejarklaustur: a tall, elderly man, extremely dynamic and one upon whom fame sits securely. He has a name for being somewhat eccentric; but he is undoubtedly a fine painter.

Reykjavík is full of interest, made all the better by the enthusiasm of Icelanders. I experienced no difficulty in gaining access to any institution which had either a municipal or national significance. There is no attempt on the part of the authorities to hide their light under a bushel. For instance, as soon as Professor Matthias Thordarson found I was interested in antiquities, he flung wide open the door of the National Museum and personally conducted me through it, taking care that I did not miss a single item that might throw light upon his country and its people.

It was similar with the educational authorities. I had heard that two new schools were being built in Reykjavík, embodying the latest architectural improvements in school buildings, while the same principle had been adopted in regard to the educational system, including up-to-date class-rooms and special amenities which none but the experienced educationalist would be aware of. The Government were spending a large sum of money on the erection of first-class schools wherever they were needed. I was surprised at what I saw in the school just being completed, and still more in the one that had but recently been begun. The almost finished school was for children between the ages of seven and twelve; the other for older and more advanced scholars.

They comprised class-rooms for not more than thirty pupils, as Icelanders are strictly against overcrowded classes; teachers' rest-rooms, a library for teachers and a museum and concert-room for the children, equipped with a stage and cinema; all lit with fluorescent lighting. A doctor, dentist and nurse always to be on the premises, the dentist's room being equipped with the most modern apparatus. There was a room fitted up with Finsen Rays apparatus. Finsen was an Icelander, although he is often called a Dane.

Attached to this school was accommodation for twenty-four children whose health would not permit them to travel to and from school. The equipment was very fine, the dormitories being fitted up with two-tiered bunks; close by was an attractive dining-room and a reading-room.

In the basement was a splendid gymnasium with accommodation for the parents in the gallery. In addition, every child must be taught swimming, and none is allowed to leave school until awarded a certificate of merit. In this way it is hoped to reduce the casualties caused by accidents at sea among the fishing population. Both of these new schools are built of an absorbent stone, resembling soap-stone, to reduce noise. On entering school every child will be compelled to change its shoes. All education is free.

The inhabitants of a country which has no mansions and no slums and where all men are equal, might well be different from other people who enjoy the doubtful advantages of modern civilisation. A people who have been so effectively cut off from the rest of the civilised world for so long, must have some characteristics peculiar to themselves. I looked for them, but failed to find anything profoundly different. They struck me as being very like ourselves but with less reserve, although they have reticence enough, a well-balanced diffidence as it were. For example, an Icelander might well be mistaken for the most tacit of men till he had been introduced and feels that he will not intrude if he speaks. He then may prove to be very talkative. In this respect they resembled Americans except that Americans are less reserved.

One can therefore endorse the opinion expressed by Lord Bryce in 1872: "The average Icelander is more talkative than the average Briton." He found him cheerful, good humoured but wanting in dash and vigour, and in the spirit of enterprise generally. He also found him apathetic and slow to make decisions; therefore very unlike his Viking ancestors. There has apparently taken place as great a change in the Icelanders' dash, vigour and ability to make decisions today as there has in his political power. My impression of the modern Icelander is that it would be difficult to find his superior in business acumen anywhere. Nor is there anything apathetic about him. The greatest trouble most foreigners meet with today when selling goods in Iceland is to stop customers making quick decisions. From what I heard, any salesman can dispose of his stock in a few minutes to the first buyer, obviously because the Icelander is anxious to corner the market to his own advantage.

Bryce found manners simple in Iceland "because there was really no distinction of rank. Nobody is rich and hardly anybody abjectly poor; everybody has to work for himself, and works . . . with his own hands." He found that wealth was not greatly coveted, and in consequence an air of cheerfulness prevailed everywhere. In those days in Iceland there was little that wealth could buy outside of absolute necessities and the indispensable comforts of a normal household. It is much the same today with the exception that wealth is more sought after; but I have never been in the home of an Icelander—and I have been in the homes of some of the wealthiest—which was better furnished than a good middle-class home in Britain. No Icelander goes in for a very large house. They have learned that apart from pandering to vanity they cause unnecessary labour and expense. Nor does there seem any likelihood that this point of view will alter.

In Bryce's day there was scarcely any difference between the farmer and the farm servant, who might end in marrying the farmer's daughter. It is still the same. There is no society in Iceland in the same sense as there is in England, France or Germany. There are no "county people,"no "four hundred," no "best sets," and therefore no struggle to get into them. This is, of course, somewhat different from the old days when the jarls still felt the effects of the social distinction they had been accustomed to in Norway, and often in Ireland and Scotland. They brought over with them their slaves; but gradually the slave element has died down and the Viking sense of personal worth and love of freedom survived.

In 1914, the American Russell, described Icelanders as "kindly, honest and hospitable;" while the Swede, Lindroth, writing in 1937, referred to them as possessing excellent physical constitutions, a rich cultural heritage, and an intellectual approach. This last trait I can thoroughly endorse, as I had occasion to present to them points of view which most people approach emotionally; but Icelanders were always calculative, logical and some coldly scientific when it came to a show down. But they never lost their natural sympathy and breadth of outlook which undoubtedly makes them, from a religious point of view, the broadest-minded and most tolerant people in the world. It is not possible to speak thus of every member of the race, but undoubtedly this criticism applies to the majority.

Let me quote one more writer who personally visited Iceland, in this case in 1856. Lord Dufferin, Governor-General of Canada, regarded them as "the most devout, innocent, pure-hearted people in the world." Today there is practically no crime in Iceland, although they, themselves, admit they are litigious.

Among the interesting features that one meets when travelling in a foreign land are the differences of food. I have already mentioned skyr, Icelandic sweet soups, and their special way of preparing mutton so that it resembles in appearance and taste nothing so much as the bottom piece of a flitch of bacon with hind leg, known as gammon. Another popular dish, and one which I cannot say I enjoyed, is sun-dried fish eaten with butter. It is tough and tasty and picked or torn apart with the fingers, and is somewhat trying to the teeth. It is a very old dish, and chiefly composed of cod, haddock, sea-wolf and halibut. Icelanders are past-masters at treating fish in different ways with a view to preserving it or making it more palatable, and a great deal is exported in these prepared forms. They refer to it as "new," "chilled," "salted" and "dried." One often sees fish being dried either by lying on the ground, or more often hung in cross-pieces high in the air, so that the wind and air can react upon it unimpeded. I often saw this operation when travelling from Reykjavík to Hafnarfjördur.

I left Iceland before the winter came, but several times passed the spot most famous for skiing, and more than once dined at the splendid guest-house built in Norwegian style for the skiers. The interior is plainer than the exterior would lead one to expect, but everything is done to whet the appetite of the skiers, even to having painted on the walls pictures depicting exciting snow scenes. The last time I passed this guest-house was after a fruitless trip to Reykir to see the small geysir Grýta; but she failed to manifest and we did not feel like waiting the hour or so before she would shoot again. Grýta has been described by one wag as "a sweet little thing, so slim and girlish." It is much smaller than Great Geysir.

One would expect there would be a lot of skiing and skating in Iceland; but certainly this is not true of the south and south-west areas. So seldom is the lake at Reykjavík frozen over that the people get insufficient practice to become proficient at the art, and an ice-rink has been opened!

Among the surprises that befell me was the unexpected appearance, while walking down the street in which I resided, of Snaefellsjökull, a charming glacier standing on the tip of Snaefellsnes, some hundreds of kilometres to the north-west. On this occasion it seemed to be at the end of the street. This phenomenon occurred on two occasions only, showing how great can be the atmospheric changes of Iceland. Normally the glacier was almost invisible from where I lived except on very clear days. Another unexpected phenomenon for which I felt very grateful was the appearance of the aurora borealis one night in August. I had just come out of a cinema about an hour before midnight when my attention was attracted by the strangely beautiful state of what I thought were clouds. Then I noticed that this particular one hung from the heavens like a frilled ribbon, and was in a constant state of motion, scintillating with the colours of the rainbow. It was a most unusual occurrence for that time of the year, as the aurora borealis is a winter phenomenon. It lasted for several hours, growing, after a time, fainter and fainter, until it finally vanished.

The summer of 1946 was unusually fine, and was followed by a winter milder than any for about seventy-five years. This synchronised with a correspondingly bad summer and winter in Britain. It was as if the zone of weather common to the northern hemisphere had dropped much farther south, leaving plenty of sun for Iceland, and doling out clouds, wind and cold for countries usually much more fortunate. The good weather was somewhat counterbalanced by Hekla erupting fiercely in the Spring of 1947, doing considerable damage. It is difficult to account for these climatic vagaries, but one way and another Nature seems intent on taking some sort of payment for whatever blessings she confers in this matter of climate.

If Iceland continues to be favoured as she had been during the last few years, there will be very little emigration. In the past the population has been terribly reduced by large numbers emigrating to Canada and the United States of America. There are at least 30,000 Icelanders in Canada and about 12,000 in the United States. It is computed that thirty per cent. of the population migrated to the Canadas between 1870-1900.

My time for departure was rapidly approaching, and it was with deep regret that I left this charming and inspiring land, and said farewell to the many Icelanders who had extended to me their hospitality and friendship. I left no country more reluctantly. The trip by air from Reykjavík to Prestwick, a distance of 844 miles, was accomplished in the remarkably short time of four hours fifteen minutes! Compare this with the four and a half days it took me to sail from Leith to Reykjavík through a stormy sea, and it will readily be seen how great the advantage of air travelling is. From Prestwich I took the train to Edinburgh, eighty-three miles away, and it took no less than six hours! To make matters more exasperating, this short journey, owing to the bad railway arrangements, compelled me to hire three taxis and five porters. I found there was nothing ususual in this, and that this form of purgatory must be endured by all who arrive at Prestwich in the evening and aspire to reach the capital city of Scotland the same day.